Marmalade

SWEET AND SAVORY SPREADS

for a Sophisticated Taste

Elizabeth Field

PHOTOGRAPHS BY HÉLÈNE DUJARDIN

Running Press
PHILADELPHIA · LONDON

ISBN 978-0-7624-4304-8
Library of Congress Control Number: 2011938662
E-book ISBN 978-0-7624-4685-8

9 8 7 6 5 4 3 2 1
Digit on the right indicates the number of this printing

Book design by Amanda Richmond
Edited by Kristen Green Wiewora
Typography: Samantha, Archive Tinted, and Carton

Running Press Book Publishers
2300 Chestnut Street
Philadelphia, PA 19103-4371

Visit us on the web!
www.runningpresscooks.com

THIS BOOK IS DEDICATED TO

Bruce & Joanna

**FOR THEIR ENDLESS SUPPORT,
PATIENCE, HUMOR, AND LOVE.**

Contents

Acknowledgments

THIS BOOK WOULD NOT BE POSSIBLE WITHOUT ELLEN FLANAGAN'S very professional and invaluable assistance on the recipes, as well as her pitch-perfect palate and creativity. Nor would it be possible without the Scottish and English home marmalade makers who responded to my original newspaper query and planted the seed for this book. Thanks to Jill Roberts for critiquing the recipes, to Trudy Ames, Amy Mato, Sam Semchenko, Helene Verin, and Joe Wheaton for their support. Huge thanks to Lynda Richardson, who commissioned and edited the original marmalade entry for the *New York Times* Topics. I am especially indebted to Barbara Ketcham Wheaton for her guidance, wisdom, and wit in her capacity as supervisor of my master's dissertation, from which this cookbook evolved; and to Anne Cleary for her early and ongoing encouragement. Thanks to the librarians at the Schlesinger Library at the Radcliffe Institute for Advanced Study, for their help with research. I could not have done this book without my agent, Sharon Bowers; my editor, Kristen Green Wiewora; and my friend, Debbie Gardner, who brought all of us together. And last but not least, extra thanks to my entire family for their enthusiasm and love.

Introduction

WHEN I WAS GROWING UP OUTSIDE NEW YORK CITY, THERE WAS always a curious container of Keiller's Scottish marmalade in our family's refrigerator. "Curious" because the jar was made of heavy white stoneware, unlike ordinary clear glass jam jars. Curious also because, compared with my favorite sweet raspberry jam, the spread was sharp and sticky with chunks of bitter orange peel. While I found it quite repulsive and avoided it like the plague, my parents happily slathered their toast and English muffins with butter, then piled on the marmalade.

Fast-forward twenty years later; as a food writer for the *Berkshire Eagle* in Pittsfield, Massachusetts, I was invited to the home of a neighbor in nearby Columbia County, New York, to sample some of his homemade marmalade. It was a frigid January day with sun bouncing off the icicles. His low-ceilinged farmhouse smelled of oranges and sugar; the fire was lit and the windows were steamy with vapors rising from a large preserving pan of bubbling liquid. Freshly filled jars of marmalade stood amber on the countertop.

David worked from scratch: He procured the knobbly, thick-skinned Seville oranges from a specialty grocery (these oranges are only available for a few short weeks in midwinter); hand sliced the peels into thin shreds; boiled water, sugar, and orange peels together until they achieved a "set"; then carefully filled and labeled his marmalade jars. He served his preserve in the classic British manner:

with crisp toast and porous crumpets anointed with butter and topped with sweet-sharp marmalade, accompanied by cups of Darjeeling tea with milk. It was a gustatory revelation.

My marmalade "epiphany" sparked my interest in learning more about the preserve from people who consider marmalade an indispensable part of their daily life. I placed a notice in a national Scottish newspaper asking for readers' marmalade recipes, tips, anecdotes, lore, and memories. I received a trove of material in letters—the Internet was in its infancy as a communication tool—from Scotland, Northern Ireland, and England, many in the spidery handwriting of the elderly.

That February I ventured forth to meet some of these individuals. My travels took me to the windswept Isle of Bute—a Glasgow taxi driver told me that his wife was an expert marmalade maker and invited me to the couple's home—to inner-city Glasgow, the snow-dusted Highlands, rolling Fife, and elegant Edinburgh. Then, driving for the first time on the "wrong" side of the road, I headed south to England, to Blackpool, Manchester, and Carlisle. I was plied with food, tea, and conversation, as well as being the recipient of multiple jars of marmalade that clanked together in my suitcase.

Since then, my interest in marmalade has grown. From books and by trial and error, I learned how to make marmalade. I attended marmalade festivals in England and Canada, and tasted marmalade everywhere I went. As I learned more about marmalade's evolution from an ancient Greek medicine to a medieval European aphrodisiac to finally an iconic British breakfast spread that traveled across the world with British colonists, I came to see marmalade as a symbol of "home." I wrote my master's dissertation on the subject.

Marmalade delights me in its uniqueness—no two jars are ever alike. Bubbling reassuringly on the stove, it celebrates the return of Seville oranges each winter and the advent of other seasonal orchard and garden bounty during the rest of the year. It inspires talk and argument among its proponents, perfumes a room and soothes the spirit, and humbly makes something delicious out of the part of the fruit that most people throw away—the peel.

Please join me in my toast to marmalade. This book has been a joy in its making, tasting, and shaping. I hope you enjoy it, too.

CHAPTER 1
Before You Start

MARMALADE IS TYPICALLY DEFINED AS A CLEAR, SWEETENED jelly in which pieces of citrus fruit and fruit peel are suspended. However, the term *marmalade* can also refer to almost any sweetened, noncitrus fruit preserve as well as savory reductions or garnishes made from vegetables or meat.

In fact, the English food writer May Byron (1861–1936) wrote in *May Byron's Jam Book* (1917): "After long and careful investigation, I find it impossible to differentiate between jams and marmalades. If any recipe calls a thing jam, marmalade, or preserve, I shall follow suit. By that or any other name, 'twill taste as sweet."

the ZEN of MARMALADE

THERE IS NO RIGHT OR WRONG WAY OF MAKING MARMALADE. SOME people use a "whole-fruit" method, in which the entire fruit is boiled in water before being combined with an equal weight of sugar and an equal weight of water, or a "cut-rind" technique, in which the peels are removed, sliced, and boiled before being added to the remaining fruit pulp and sugar. Some people prepare their marmalade in a pressure cooker or use premade marmalade mixtures on which to base their preserves. Some cut their fruit by hand; others use a food processor. Still others warm their sugar in the oven before combining it with fruit, or presoak their fruit overnight before boiling it, for added tenderness.

The point is that citrus fruit contains an abundance of natural acid and pectin, which, in interaction with sugar and heat, causes jams and jellies to set. This allows for greater flexibility in technique than does jam making with low-pectin, low-acid fruits such as strawberries, raspberries, pears, rhubarb, and peaches. These jams often require supplemental pectin, in the form of a liquid extract made from boiling other fruits with water, or commercial pectin, made from dehydrated citrus pith. (No recipes in this book call for either of these supplements.)

Please feel free to make minor adjustments in the sugar content of these recipes, according to your personal preference. And you can slice or dice your fruit rinds in any thickness or shape that you like. Similarly, marmalade is so forgiving that you can decide not to warm the sugar, as indicated in some recipes, without any problem at all.

WHAT *You* NEED

SMALL BATCHES OF MARMALADE ARE MUCH EASIER TO WORK WITH than large batches. You will need a heavy, 4- or 5-quart/3^3/$_4$- or 4^3/$_4$-liter saucepan and lid with a diameter of at least 8 inches/20 centimeters. Small and medium saucepans are helpful, too, for intermediary cooking processes or for very small batches of marmalade. Heavy-gauge aluminum with nonstick interiors, anodized metals such as Calphalon, enameled steel, enameled iron, and stainless steel all work fine. Tin-lined copper preserving pans are lovely to use, but they are quite expensive. Do not use unlined aluminum, copper, iron, or tin pans, as they can cause fruit to oxidize. A pan that is wider than it is deep is great for marmalade making because it allows the liquid from the boiling fruit to evaporate quickly. Whatever saucepan you use should have a capacity of at least four times that of the food to be cooked in it, as marmalades can foam up and boil over, creating a nasty cleanup job on your stovetop. If you own and like to use a pressure cooker, fine, but pressure cookers are entirely optional equipment.

You will need a kitchen scale for weighing fruit and sugar. I use a mechanical scale, but various digital models at different price points are available.

A candy or sugar thermometer graduated to 400°F/205°C is essential for precise monitoring of the temperature of your boiling marmalade, which will achieve a set at 220°F/106°C. Do not substitute a meat thermometer for a candy thermometer, because the increments on a meat thermometer are not small enough to use for measuring sugar temperatures.

- Wooden spoons
- Graduated measuring spoons
- Liquid and dry measuring cups
- Large colander or strainer
- Stainless-steel ladle
- Stainless-steel skimmer
- Stainless-steel tongs or jar lifter
- Jam funnel
- Stainless-steel zester
- Sharp chef's knife
- Sharp paring knife

- Vegetable peeler
- Citrus squeezer
- Fine sieve
- Cheesecloth
- Kitchen towels
- Mixing bowls
- Rubber gloves
- Canning jars with lids
- Labels
- Food processor (optional)

PREPARING *Your* FRUIT

THERE ARE VARIOUS METHODS OF MAKING MARMALADE, INCLUDING
Whole-Fruit Seville Orange Marmalade (page 36), in which oranges are boiled whole before being combined with an equal weight of sugar and water, and Cut-Rind Seville Orange Marmalade (page 39), where the peels are removed, sliced, and boiled before being added to the fruit pulp, sugar, and water.

Always start with the freshest—preferably organic—fruit that you can find. Farmers' markets are a good place to find seasonal tree fruit, such as apples, pears, and peaches, and, if you are lucky enough to live in an orange-growing region, fresh citrus fruit. Wash all fruit carefully before using, even if it is organic.

Citrus fruits are often covered in a preservative wax; removing it is essential. To do so, rinse the fruit thoroughly under warm running water to remove surface dirt. Gently scrub the peel with a clean scrub brush; then rinse again under warm water. Dry with a kitchen towel. If any preservative wax remains, fill a basin with boiling water. Plunge the fruit in, and you will notice an oily residue floating to the surface. Remove the fruit and rinse under warm running water. I have been told that spraying white vinegar on citrus fruit removes waxy residues. Be sure to rinse well after spritzing the fruit. Produce washing products are also available in supermarkets.

Hand cutting citrus peels can be laborious. Use sharp knives, and always allot plenty of time for the task, so that it won't be an ordeal. Some marmalade makers use food processors to slice their peels; I prefer hand cutting as you can achieve the exact size and thickness that you wish.

Pectin is the substance in fruit and berries that combines with sugar and acid to make jams, jellies, preserves, and marmalades gel. Citrus fruit contains an abundance of natural pectin; it is concentrated in the fruit's pith and seeds. Some recipes in this book call for preparing a 12-inch/30-centimeter square of double-thickness cheesecloth, in which to enclose seeds and pith. The bag is boiled along with the fruit, and discarded before adding sugar. This step maximizes your marmalade's pectin content.

TO SOAK or NOT to SOAK

MANY TRADITIONAL RECIPES FOR ORANGE MARMALADE CALL FOR soaking the citrus peels overnight or longer. This is said to soften the peels. Although technically it is not necessary to presoak the peels, be sure that you have boiled them until they are easily pierced with a fork before adding sugar. Once you have added sugar, the peels will not change in texture.

STERILIZING JARS

TO ENSURE A TIGHT SEAL, JARS SHOULD BE IN PERFECT, UNCHIPPED condition. Quarter-pint, half-pint, and pint-size canning jars are available in your local grocery store or hardware store. They are remarkably inexpensive. I like the standard plain glass jars available in various sizes, as well as the hexagonal glass jars available from Specialty Bottle, at www.specialtybottle.com. To sterilize jars and covers, wash them in hot, soapy water, then rinse. Air-dry on a kitchen towel until the marmalade is ready to be processed. While the marmalade is cooking, fill a large stockpot with water and bring to a boil. Place a canning rack or folded kitchen towel on the bottom of a large stockpot: This prevents the jars from rattling against one another. (If you have an old-fashioned round cooling rack that fits in your pot, you can also use that.) Use a jar lifter or tongs to add your clean jars to the pot as the water is coming to a boil, to sterilize them. Leave enough room between each jar for water to circulate freely, and allow 1 inch/2.5 centimeters of water above the tops of the jars. Boil for 10 minutes. In a small saucepan, simmer the jar lids in a small amount of water to soften the rubber flange around the edge. Remove and drain the hot, sterilized jars and lids.

FILLING *the* JARS

WHEN THE MARMALADE HAS REACHED ITS SETTING POINT OF 220°F/ 104°C, as mentioned earlier, I check for a firm set, using both a candy thermometer and the "wrinkle test." Simply put a teaspoon or so of boiling marmalade on a cold saucer; then place in the freezer for 5 minutes. Remove the saucer from the freezer and press the surface of the marmalade with your thumb. If it wrinkles, the marmalade is ready.

Allow it to stand for 5 to 10 minutes before pouring it into jars. As it cools slightly, the jelly around the fruit begins to set, which will prevent the peel from sinking to the bottom. Remove your jars from the pot with a jar lifter or tongs, dumping the boiling water back into the pot. Set them on a folded kitchen towel on the counter right-side up; the heat from the glass will cause the water to evaporate. Never place jars directly on a solid metal surface, where thermal shock might crack them. Use a ladle and a jar funnel to fill the jars, leaving a $^1/_4$-inch/6-millimeter headspace. Wipe off any drips with a damp kitchen towel. Cover each jar with a lid and tighten a metal band around it. Don't screw it on with great force: just tight enough to close the jar. (From the time you remove the jars from the hot water until you fill and process them, you should move quickly. If the jars or their contents cool down before they hit the boiling water, the jars could break in the pot.)

WATER-BATH PROCESSING

THE U.S. DEPARTMENT OF AGRICULTURE AND STATE COOPERATIVE Extension Agents recommend water-bath processing as a safety precaution for preserving and pickling all acid fruits and vegetables.

To process, place a rack or a folded kitchen towel on the bottom of a very large steel or enameled pot, or canner. Fill halfway with water. Heat the water to 180°F/82°C. Use a jar lifter to set your filled and sealed jars in the hot water in the pot. Add more hot water so that the jars are covered by 2 inches/5 centimeters of water above the lids with 1 to 2 inches/2.5 to 5 centimeters to the top of the pot to allow for splashes. The water should circulate freely among the jars. Bring the water to a boil over high heat. Set your timer and maintain a steady boil for 5 minutes. Immediately transfer the jars to a counter covered with a kitchen towel, and let cool completely to room temperature. Check the seals by removing the metal bands and lifting up on the lids; if they hold fast, the seals are good, and the jars can be stored outside the refrigerator. Any jars that did not seal can be stored in the refrigerator. When the jars are completely cool, wait 24 hours before retightening the lids. Label them, and store them in a cool, dry place, out of bright light.

NOTE: I do not always process my marmalade in a water bath. The high sugar and acid content in marmalade retards bacteria, and thus lessens the chances of spoilage. As long as my jars and lids are meticulously sterilized and properly sealed, I am comfortable.

STORAGE *and* SPOILAGE

IDEALLY, MARMALADE SHOULD BE STORED IN A COOL, DARK PLACE FOR at least one month before consuming, to maximize the balance of flavors (though it's understandable if you want to sample your marmalade before then). Most marmalades should be consumed within one year, although many experienced marmalade makers believe that marmalade actually improves with time. (Some commercial marmalade makers sell "aged" or "vintage" marmalade.)

Some of the recipes in this book, particularly for noncitrus marmalades, do not entail water-bath processing, and are not designed to be kept for more than a week or so in the refrigerator. However, most opened jars of marmalade do keep very well in the refrigerator.

Mold may appear if marmalade is kept for long periods. Contrary to earlier beliefs that mold was fairly harmless, some molds produce mycotoxins that can be harmful if eaten. A bit of mold on the top of an open jar should not be scooped off and ignored; discard the product. If refrigerated marmalade crystallizes, place the jar in a saucepan of water (about halfway up the sides of the jar) and heat gently until the marmalade liquefies again. If you eat marmalade only occasionally, try canning it in quarter-pint jars, which hold only a few servings.

PACKAGING

THERE ARE INFINITE WAYS OF PRESENTING YOUR JARS OF MARMALADE.
An attractive square of cloth placed over the lid, secured with a rubber band, and then tied with a decorative ribbon looks polished and appealing. Burlap is wonderful for a country look. There are many websites where you can order personalized labels, or you can make them yourself. It's always nice to include the name of your marmalade, the maker's name, the ingredients, and the date it was made, on the label.

TROUBLESHOOTING

IF YOUR MARMALADE WON'T SET, TRY REBOILING IT BRISKLY FOR 2
minutes. Chill a spoonful of it in the freezer for a few minutes; if it shows signs of improvement, boil for a minute or so longer, or until it tests done. Pour into sterilized containers, seal, and process in a hot water bath for 5 minutes (page 16). Do not work with more than 4 cups/950 milliliters at a time.

Stiff, overcooked marmalades can be fixed by either melting them down with a little water or fruit juice, or combining them with an uncooked batch and boiling until it thickens to the proper consistency.

If your citrus peels are tough, you haven't precooked them long enough before combining them with sugar. This is why many marmalade makers soak their peels in water overnight to soften them. You can't change the texture of the peel once you have added the sugar.

HIGH-ALTITUDE CONSIDERATIONS

AT HIGH ALTITUDES, WATER BOILS AT A LOWER TEMPERATURE THAN AT sea level. To compensate for lost heat, increase the water-bath processing time from 5 to 10 minutes at altitudes of 1,000 feet/305 meters above sea level to 6,000 feet/1,829 meters above sea level. Increase the processing time to 15 minutes at altitudes above 6,000 feet/1,829 meters.

At altitudes above 1,000 feet/305 meters, increase the headspace in your filled jars from $^1/_4$ inch/6 millimeters to $^1/_2$ inch/1.3 centimeters.

INGREDIENTS

THE PRIMARY INGREDIENTS IN MARMALADE ARE CITRUS OR OTHER fruit and sugar. As in all simple dishes, choose the finest, freshest (preferably organic) ingredients you can find. Always wash your produce (even if it is organic) before using it.

Following are some of the ingredients you'll encounter while making marmalade, and what to look for when purchasing them.

APPLES. Avoid fruit with blemishes and bruises. Summer varieties are usually tarter than those harvested in the fall. If you live in an apple-growing region, pick your own!

CHILES. Varieties range from mildly hot to scorching. Always wear rubber gloves when preparing chiles, as their oils can be irritating to the skin.

CITRONS. Larger and more elongated than lemons, these fruit range in color from green to yellow to orange. They are composed mostly of peel, $^1\!/_2$ inch/1.3 centimeters thick or more, and dozens of seeds.

GRAPEFRUITS. Grapefruits are available year-round, but they are at their best during the winter months. Choose a fruit that is heavy for its size; this indicates juiciness.

GINGER. Fresh ginger should be firm and fresh, with no wrinkling of the skin. It keeps well, peeled and wrapped in plastic, in the freezer. Ginger is easily grated while frozen.

KUMQUATS. Bright orange and about the size and shape of an olive, the entire kumquat is edible, including the thin, soft peel.

LEMONS. Choose lemons that give easily to gentle pressure, indicating a thin peel and plenty of juice. For marmalades using whole fruit, select rough-skinned lemons that are quite firm, indicating a thick peel and less juice. Meyer lemons are smaller, sweeter, rounder, milder, and less acidic than conventional lemons. Their peel may be pale orange in color. They are available between December and April in specialty markets.

LIMES. Limes should have a bright green peel, with no soft, yellowish spots indicating over-ripeness. When cooked, their peels turn a muddy brownish-green, which is why I do not include any recipes for lime marmalade. Instead, I use lime zest as a zippy flavoring in other marmalades.

ORANGES. There are four main types of orange in cultivation. Seville (bitter) oranges are large, spheroid, and very seedy, with an extremely bitter peel and flesh. Grown predominantly in Spain and California, these oranges are used in proper British-style marmalade. Seville oranges are available for just a few weeks—usually from mid-January to mid-February. Because of their scarcity, you can buy them in bulk and freeze them in a plastic bag for several months. Look for them in specialty markets; ask your produce manager if they can be special ordered. Common sweet oranges include the Valencia, which has a thin, bright orange peel, usually two to four seeds, plenty of juice, and a pleasant, sweet flavor. Navel oranges are typically large, very sweet, richly flavored, and seedless, with a characteristic "baby" fruit embedded in its apex. Blood oranges have mottled red and orange peels, produced by a mutation that probably occurred in the seventeenth century in Sicily. The flesh is dark and magenta colored, with an aromatic, perfumelike flavor. They are grown primarily in the Mediterranean region, and are available in February and March. All oranges keep well in the refrigerator for several weeks.

PEACHES. I prefer yellow peaches, as they are less delicate than white peaches, which can be overpowered by citrus fruit. Select peaches that are firm and unbruised (avoid ones with a mushy or mealy texture), and taste for sweetness and juiciness before using in marmalades or any other dish.

PASSION FRUITS. These fruits have a tart flavor and floral fragrance that blends extremely well with citrus fruit.

PEARS. Choose fruit that are ripe but firm. Varieties range in color from pale green to golden yellow to barn red to russet brown.

QUINCES. Quinces are far too astringent to be eaten raw. When cooked, their flesh turns a lovely rose color, and their flavor is tart but aromatic. Quinces are available in early to late fall.

RHUBARB. Rhubarb must be cooked, not eaten raw. For marmalades, the palest pink varieties are best, even pale pink, tinged with green. Choose stalks that are neither too thin nor too thick; avoid wilted stalks. Their season is early spring to late summer.

TANGERINES. Choose bright orange fruit that are heavy for their size.

TOMATILLOS. Also known as Mexican green tomatoes or husk tomatoes, tomatillos range in diameter from 1 to 2 inches/2.5 to 5 centimeters, and are enclosed in a papery husk. They are available year-round in Hispanic markets.

TOMATOES. The best tomatoes are firm, plump, and free from blemishes. Home-grown and farmers' market tomatoes explode with flavor in late summer; avoid their pale, cottony-textured, out-of-season counterparts.

VANILLA BEANS. Long, slender, dark brown, and grown in Africa, Mexico, Tahiti, and other tropical locales, vanilla beans should have an intense aroma and feel oily to the touch. Both the seeds and entire pod are rich in flavor. Substitute a high-quality pure vanilla extract for vanilla beans.

YUZU. This orange, golf ball–size citrus hybrid has a distinctive floral aroma and a lemon-lime flavor. Native to Japan, it can be difficult to obtain in the United States, but can sometimes be found in Asian supermarkets.

SUGAR AND OTHER FLAVORINGS

MOST OF THE RECIPES IN THIS BOOK CALL FOR GRANULATED WHITE sugar, or light or dark brown sugar. Feel free to substitute natural cane sugar, which has a slightly cleaner taste than processed white sugar does.

Wine, whiskey, brandy, and flavored liqueurs add depth and complexity to marmalade. Stir them in once the marmalade has reached its setting point, as cooking will evaporate the alcohol and flavor.

CHAPTER 2

TRADITIONAL *Marmalade* FLAVORS

MARMALADE ORIGINATED MORE THAN TWO THOUSAND YEARS ago as a solid cooked quince and honey paste similar to today's membrillo, the Spanish quince paste that is typically served with sheep's milk cheeses. Known as *melomeli* in ancient Greece and *melimela* in Latin, it was used both as a preserve and a reputed remedy for digestive complaints. The Portuguese took up the product, perhaps via the Arabs, substituting sugar for honey, around the tenth century. They called it *marmelada*, which derives from the Portuguese *marmelo*, or quince.

The first shipments of *marmelada*, packed in wooden boxes, arrived in London in 1495. Fabulously expensive and imbued with purported medical and aphrodisiac powers, it was a popular gift among noble families.

A northern European version of a cooked quince and sugar preserve called alternately chardequince, condoignac, cotignac, or quiddony sprang up. Flavored with red wine, honey, cinnamon stick, and powdered ginger, it was taken at the end of a medieval feast, along with pears, nuts, sugar-coated aniseed, and other sweetmeats whose purpose, harkening back to the ancient Greeks, was to ease an upset stomach.

Versions of quince marmalade made by country gentlewomen adorned the elegant sweetmeats tables displayed at the end of sixteenth- and seventeenth-century English feasts. Rolled and twisted into hearts and knots or flattened and then stamped with designs such as flowers or animals, both white and rose-colored quince pastes were as decorative as they were therapeutic.

Membrillo

THIS RECIPE FOR A SLIGHTLY TART, ROSE-COLORED, SOLID QUINCE
paste harkens back to the earliest forms of marmalade, called marmelada, *made in
eleventh-century Spain. Membrillo is still quite popular in Spain, Portugal, and Latin
America, where it typically accompanies sheep's milk cheeses or is used in pastries. Membrillo has a following among American food lovers, too. Available at specialty cheese
shops, it looks and tastes lovely, sliced, on any cheese tray, either as an hors d'oeuvre or for
dessert. You can make a quick healthy snack by spreading cream cheese on a water
cracker and topping it with a dab of membrillo. Here's the homemade version, for anyone
who has access to fresh quinces during their season in autumn.*

YIELDS ABOUT 2½ CUPS/590 MILLILITERS

4 large quinces

Juice of 1 lemon

Granulated sugar

Wash the quinces and rub off the fuzzy down that usually covers their skin.
Peel and quarter, but do not core them. Place the quinces in a medium, heavy-
bottomed saucepan and add cold water to cover them by about ½ inch/1.3
centimeters, about 4½ cups/1 liter. Add the lemon juice. Bring to a boil, then
lower the heat to medium-low and simmer uncovered, stirring occasionally,
for 2 hours.

The consistency will be like that of chunky applesauce. Add additional water if the mixture is in any danger of drying out.

Drain, reserving the liquid. Remove the cores and seeds, and discard. Mash the fruit into a rough purée.

Weigh the purée on a kitchen scale, and measure out an equal weight of sugar. Return the liquid to the saucepan and reduce it to about $^3/_4$ cup/178 milliliters. Add the purée and sugar to the saucepan. Over very low heat, allow the sugar to dissolve. Cook, stirring often with a wooden spoon and making sure that the mixture doesn't burn, for about 20 minutes, or until it thickens and begins to splutter. Then stir constantly until it becomes a deep rose-colored paste that pulls away from the sides of the pan. Let cool for about 5 minutes.

Line an 11 x 8-inch/28 x 20-centimeter pan with parchment or plastic wrap. Transfer the membrillo to the pan, spreading it to a thickness of about $^3/_4$ inch/ 2 centimeters. Leave for a day or so to dry out in a warm, airy place. Turn out of the pan and cut into 2-inch/5-centimeter pieces. Serve immediately on a cheese plate, sliced thinly. Alternatively, thinly slice an individual block and store in a tin or other airtight container. Membrillo will keep for at least 2 weeks at room temperature. You can choose to roll the slices of membrillo in granulated sugar before serving, if you wish, to give it a special touch.

How Marmalade Got Its Name

LEGEND HAS IT THAT MARY, QUEEN OF SCOTS WAS OFFERED SOME quince marmalade to combat seasickness on crossing the English Channel from Calais to Scotland in 1561. She said to her servant, "Marmelade pour Marie malade," or possibly, "Marmelade pour ma maladie," which means "Quince for my malady." Some writers credited Mary for introducing marmalade into Britain, but it's more likely that the comments were an example of the type of punning the Elizabethans loved. Marmalade's name derives from *marmelada*, from *marmelo*, the Portuguese word for "quince."

Quince-Raspberry
MARMALADE

THIS RECIPE FOLLOWS THE TRADITIONAL METHOD USED BY ENGLISH *home cooks. I have added fresh raspberries, which gives this marmalade a candy-pink color and a deep floral aroma.*

YIELDS ABOUT 3 CUPS/710 MILLILITERS

4 large quinces

Juice of 1 lemon

4 cups/720 grams granulated sugar

3 cups/300 grams raspberries, washed and puréed through the fine disk of a food mill or rubbed through a fine sieve

WASH THE QUINCES and rub off the fuzzy down that usually covers their skin. Peel and quarter, and discard the core and seeds. Slice thinly.

Place the quinces in a medium, heavy-bottomed saucepan and add water to cover them by about $^1/_2$ inch/1.3 centimeters, about $4^1/_2$ cups/1 liter. Add the lemon juice. Bring to a boil, then lower the heat to medium-low and simmer uncovered, stirring occasionally, for 1½ hours. The quinces will be very soft. Add additional water if the mixture is in any danger of drying out.

Add the sugar and stir to dissolve. Add the puréed raspberries. Raise the heat to medium-high, and cook uncovered, stirring gently with a wooden spoon, for 15 to 20 minutes, or until the mixture thickens, becomes rose colored, and begins to splutter. Stir constantly until a candy thermometer reads 220°F/104°C. Use the "wrinkle test" (page 15) to double-check for a firm set. Skim off any scum. Let stand in the saucepan for 5 minutes before ladling into hot, sterilized canning jars (page 15), leaving ¼ inch/6 millimeters of headspace (page 15). Seal. Process the jars in a hot water bath for 5 minutes (page 16). When thoroughly cool, label the jars. Store in a cool, dark place.

AROMATIC
Orange-Apple-Ginger
MARMALADE

AWARD-WINNING SCOTTISH CHEF AND COOKING SCHOOL TEACHER
Mo Scott prepared this extremely satisfying marmalade for me in her cozy farm-house kitchen outside of Glasgow, Scotland. It resembles some Elizabethan marmalades, which incorporated apples and spices with oranges, before the spread evolved to "true" orange marmalades, comprised solely of oranges. Stored in a pretty jar and topped with a square of decorative fabric, this sophisticated, amber-colored marmalade makes a wonderful gift.

YIELDS ABOUT 7 CUPS/1.9 LITERS

5 Seville oranges, halved

3 pounds/1.3 kilograms Granny Smith or other cooking apples
 (about 6), peeled, cored, and quartered

$6^{1}/_{2}$ cups/1.1 kilograms granulated sugar

1 ($9^{1}/_{2}$-ounce/265-gram) jar crystallized ginger, chopped,
 with syrup reserved, or 6 ounces/180 grams chopped crystallized ginger

$1^{1}/_{2}$ tablespoons ground ginger

REMOVE THE ORANGE seeds and place them in a 12-inch/30-centimeter square of double-thickness cheesecloth. Gather up the corners and tie them shut with kitchen string. Place in a large, heavy-bottomed saucepan. Scoop out the orange pulp with a spoon and place in the saucepan. Scrape away the white pith with a knife and discard. Slice the orange peels into $^1/_4$-inch-wide/6 millimeter-wide strips. Place in the saucepan. Add $1^1/_2$ quarts/1.4 liters of water. Soak overnight.

Over high heat, bring the orange mixture to a boil. Reduce the heat to medium-low and simmer for 1 to $1^1/_2$ hours, or until the orange peel is very tender when pierced with a fork. Discard the cheesecloth bag.

Place the apple quarters and $^1/_2$ cup/120 milliliters of water in a medium, heavy-bottomed saucepan. Cook, partially covered, over medium-low heat, stirring until the apples and water dissolve into a purée. Watch carefully that the purée doesn't burn, and if necessary add more water. Stir the apple purée into the orange mixture.

Stir in the sugar, crystallized ginger, its reserved syrup or $^1/_2$ cup/118 millimeters of water, and the ground ginger. Bring the mixture to a boil and stir until the sugar dissolves. Taste and add additional sugar if you prefer a sweeter marmalade. Reduce the heat to medium-low and simmer, stirring occasionally, for 35 to 45 minutes, or until a candy thermometer reads 220°F/104°C. Use the "wrinkle test" (page 15) to double-check for a firm set. Skim off any scum. Let stand in the saucepan for 5 minutes before ladling into hot, sterilized canning jars (page 15), leaving $^1/_4$ inch/ 6 millimeters of headspace (page 15). Seal. Process the jars in a hot water bath for 5 minutes (page 16). When thoroughly cool, label the jars. Store in a cool, dark place.

CHAPTER 3

CITRUS *Marmalades*

I N THE EIGHTEENTH CENTURY, THE SCOTS PIONEERED THE SWITCH-over from quince to orange marmalade. Many regions of the country were too cold for quince trees to grow, and imported Seville (bitter) oranges had been popular among the wealthy since the late fifteenth century. Cooks were now producing a thinner form of marmalade, stored in pots or glasses, achieved through a shorter cooking time.

Just as important was a new consumption pattern, whereby marmalade was eaten at breakfast instead of after dinner. Still considered a healthful "restorative," it became a ubiquitous part of the British breakfast.

Legend goes that in the late eighteenth century, a grocer's wife, Janet Keiller, bought a load of Seville oranges cheaply from a storm-driven ship that had taken shelter in Dundee harbor. Janet turned the oranges into marmalade, using her husband's stock of sugar, and it sold so successfully that the firm of James Keiller and Son marmalade manufacturers was founded in 1797.

Janet probably didn't "invent" orange marmalade, but she was part of a movement of Scottish cooks responsible for turning marmalade into an art form. Refining their techniques, they produced marmalades that ranged from transparent to dark russet, contained delicate "chips" (shreds) or robust chunks, and ranged in taste from mildly sweet to quite bitter—all the textures and qualities we look for in today's marmalades. This chapter contains both traditional and more modern takes on citrus marmalade.

Whole-Fruit Seville Orange
MARMALADE

THIS RICH, DARK, ROBUST MARMALADE IS ONE OF THE EASIEST OF *all marmalades to make. Utilizing the whole-fruit method, the oranges require no initial peeling or slicing at all (if you're using frozen Seville oranges, it isn't even necessary to defrost them), but it does require a kitchen scale. This recipe employs the classic 1:1:1 ratio of fruit, water, and sugar, which you can use as a template for making any citrus marmalade. Quantities of sugar can be adjusted to your liking without affecting the set or texture of the marmalade. If you don't have Seville oranges, substitute sweet oranges (juice and Valencia oranges are less sweet than navels), and reduce the amount of sugar used by one-third to one half. Some marmalade makers prefer to warm the sugar, so that it takes less time to dissolve and less time to cook to the setting point. You may choose to also do it, or skip it.*

YIELDS ABOUT 10 CUPS/1.9 LITERS

3 pounds/1.3 kilograms (about 10) Seville oranges

Juice of 4 lemons (seeds reserved if you are using the pressure cooker variation, page 38).

Granulated sugar

PREHEAT THE OVEN to 250°F/120°C to warm the sugar (optional).

Place the whole oranges with water to cover in a large, heavy-bottomed saucepan. Cover the saucepan and simmer gently for about 1½ hours, or until the oranges are very tender when pierced with a fork.

Lift out the fruit and weigh it; reserve the cooking water. Add the lemon juice to the cooking water, then weigh out an amount of cooking water equal to the fruit. Reserve. Set aside an equal weight of sugar. Warm the sugar on a foil-lined baking sheet in the oven for 15 minutes, if you wish.

Place a cutting board on a large, rimmed baking sheet so that you don't lose any of the juice. Halve the oranges crosswise and scoop out the soft centers with a spoon. Reserve. Thinly slice or dice the peel. Remove and discard the seeds, but if you miss any, do not worry. They will float to the surface when you boil the fruit and sugar, and are easily skimmed off.

Put the sliced orange peel, the escaped juice, reserved orange pulp, cooking water, and sugar in a wide, shallow, heavy-bottomed pan. Boil briskly, uncovered, stirring to prevent sticking, for 20 to 30 minutes, or until the mixture thickens and darkens and a candy thermometer reads 220°F/104°C. Use the "wrinkle test" (page 15) to double-check for a firm set. Skim off any scum or floating seeds. Let stand in the saucepan for 5 minutes before ladling into hot, sterilized canning jars (page 15), leaving ¼ inch/6 millimeters of headspace (page 15). Seal. Process the jars in a hot water bath for 5 minutes (page 16). When thoroughly cool, label the jars. Store in a cool, dark place.

Whole-Fruit Seville Orange Variation:

PRESSURE COOKER MARMALADE

This technique comes to me via Rachael Carron, one of the owners of WD-50 restaurant in New York City. Put the whole oranges in a pressure cooker with 10 cups/2.5 liters of water. Bring up to high pressure and cook for 15 minutes. Use the quick-release method and place the oranges in a bowl to cool for a few minutes. Place the cooking liquid in a large, heavy-bottomed saucepan. Add the lemon juice.

Thinly slice or dice the oranges, and set aside. Remove the orange membranes and seeds and place in a small saucepan with the lemon seeds. Add water to cover and boil for 5 minutes. Drain the mixture through a fine sieve into the reserved orange cooking water. Work with a spatula to extract all of the gelatinous pectin into the cooking water by scraping the underside of the sieve. Discard the orange seeds and membranes.

Add the sliced oranges to the orange cooking water. Over low heat, add 6 pounds/2.7 kilograms of sugar and stir until the sugar is completely dissolved. Bring to a boil and cook briskly, until the mixture thickens and darkens and a candy thermometer reads 220ºF/104ºC. Use the "wrinkle test" (page 15) to double-check for a firm set. Let stand in the saucepan for 5 minutes before ladling into hot, sterilized canning jars (page 15), leaving $^1/_4$ inch/6 millimeters of headspace (page 15). Seal. Process the jars in a hot water bath for 5 minutes (page 16). When thoroughly cool, label the jars. Store in a cool, dark place.

Cut-Rind Seville Orange

MARMALADE

THIS RECIPE USES THE CUT-RIND METHOD OF MARMALADE MAKING, *which results in a purer fruit flavor, with a lighter color, looser texture, and clearer jelly than whole-fruit marmalade. This recipe can easily be doubled for a larger yield. Be sure to allot plenty of time for the hand slicing of citrus peels. Some marmalade makers use a food processor for this task, but I believe that hand slicing is what gives marmalade its character and individuality. This recipe can easily be halved or further reduced.*

YIELDS ABOUT 5 CUPS/1.18 LITERS

2¼ pounds/1 kilogram (about 6 to 7) Seville oranges, halved

1 large lemon, halved

Granulated sugar

JUICE THE ORANGES and the lemon, reserving the seeds. Strain the juice through a sieve and set the juice aside. Scoop the pulp from the insides, reserving with the seeds. Cut the citrus halves lengthwise into quarters, turn them peel-side down on a cutting board, and scrape away as much pith as possible with a sharp knife or vegetable peeler. (It is fine if a thin layer of pith remains.)

Discard the pith. Slice the citrus peels thinly or in small squares.

Bundle the reserved seeds and pulp into a 12-inch/30-centimeter square of double-thickness cheesecloth; tie it shut with kitchen string. Weigh the seed bundle with the chopped citrus peels; measure out an equal weight of sugar and set aside. Move the reserved juice to the scale and weigh it: add enough water to equal the weight of the sugar. The citrus peels and seeds bundle, sugar, and liquid should all measure the same weight. Combine the seed bundle, citrus peels, and liquid in a heavy saucepan.

Bring to a boil over high heat, then lower the heat and simmer covered, over low heat, stirring occasionally, for about 1 hour, or until the peel is very tender when pierced with a fork. The mixture should have reduced by about one-third.

Remove the cheesecloth bag, squeezing out any excess juice, and discard. Add the sugar and stir over low heat until it has completely dissolved. Increase the heat and boil rapidly for 15 to 20 minutes, or until a candy thermometer reads 220°F/104°C. Use the "wrinkle test" (page 15) to double-check for a firm set. Skim off any scum. Let stand in the saucepan for 5 minutes before ladling into hot, sterilized canning jars (page 15), leaving $1/4$ inch/6 millimeters of headspace (page 15). Seal. Process the jars in a hot water bath for 5 minutes (page 16). When thoroughly cool, label the jars. Store in a cool, dark place.

Variations:

TIPSY MARMALADE. Follow the recipe on page 39, and add about 1 tablespoon of whiskey, rum, or brandy per cup of marmalade after skimming it when it reaches the setting point. Let stand for 5 minutes; stir once to ensure even distribution of the alcohol.

BROWN SUGAR MARMALADE. Follow the recipe on page 39, substituting light or dark brown sugar for one-third to one-half the weight of the granulated sugar. This will produce a darker-colored and richer marmalade.

MARMALADE WITH ALMONDS. Follow the recipe on page 39 and add 1 cup/115 grams of slivered almonds after skimming the marmalade. Let stand for 5 minutes; stir once to ensure even distribution of the nuts.

NOTE: The cut-rind method is an adaptable one: If Seville oranges are not available—or if you prefer a naturally sweeter marmalade—substitute sweet oranges. Just follow this simple formula: For each pound/450 grams of Seville oranges called for, weigh the same amount of sweet oranges. Remove one of the oranges and replace with one lemon. (The lemon should be dealt with in the same way as the oranges.) Reduce the sugar by about one quarter, and then taste the mixture after the sugar has been dissolved, and add more, if you like, for additional sweetness.

Marmalade as an Aphrodisiac

IN MEDIEVAL AND ELIZABETHAN TIMES, MARMALADE WAS NOT ONLY considered medicinal but was linked with love. The playwright Philip Massinger referred in 1629 to a kiss withheld in the words, "I cannot blame my lady's unwillingness to part with such marmalade lips." It was also considered an aphrodisiac. A recipe published in 1608, laced with rare, expensive ingredients such as musk, ambergris, eringo roots (sea holly), and pearls, was given to Queen Mary in the hope that it would help her conceive a son. (It didn't.)

Similarly, heart-shaped molded marmalades that were served after feasts were associated with "marmalet madams," or sweethearts. The meaning of "marmalet madams" later changed to refer to prostitutes. Could there be any connection to Bob Crewe and Kenny Nolan's classic hit song, "Lady Marmalade," sung by Patti LaBelle, about a New Orleans prostitute, which came out about three hundred fifty years later?

Dark Bitter Orange
MARMALADE

CHUNKY, MAHOGANY-COLORED, AND WITH A STRONG, ROBUST FLA-vor, *this marmalade resembles Frank Cooper's Vintage Oxford Marmalade, a commercial English marmalade nicknamed "squish," which was a traditional favorite among Oxford University dons and undergraduates. This association, along with its texture and flavor, may have fueled its reputation as a "masculine" marmalade. (English explorer Robert Scott carried this among his provisions on his voyage to the Antarctic in 1911–12, as did Sir Edmund Hillary, when he scaled Mount Everest in 1953. Even Ian Fleming's James Bond, the epitome of English suave, has his daily breakfast regimen of a boiled egg, whole wheat toast with Jersey butter, and Frank Cooper's marmalade, with very strong coffee.) This marmalade makes a sophisticated counterpoint to the rich eggs and cream of Marmalade Ice Cream (page 144), and is great on its own with toast and butter.*

YIELDS 2 TO 3 CUPS / 475 TO 710 MILLILITERS

1 pound/450 grams (about 6) Seville oranges, halved crosswise

$1/2$ lemon

2 cups/360 grams granulated sugar

2 teaspoons blackstrap molasses

JUICE THE ORANGES and the lemon half, removing and reserving the seeds. Scrape out any visible pith and pulp with a spoon, and reserve it. Strain the juice into a large, heavy-bottomed saucepan. Coarsely cut the orange peel into either a $^1/_2$-inch/1.3-centimeter dice or short, wide strips, and add to the saucepan. Roughly chop the lemon half. Put the reserved citrus seeds, citrus pith and pulp, and the chopped lemon into a 12-inch/30 centimeter square of double-thickness cheesecloth. Gather up the corners and tie them shut with kitchen string. Add the bag to the saucepan. Add $4^1/_2$ cups/1.06 milliliters of water and bring to a boil. Reduce the heat to low and simmer for about $1^1/_2$ hours, or until the peel is tender when pierced with a fork. The mixture should have reduced by about one-third.

Lift the cheesecloth bag from the saucepan, and when it is cool enough to handle, squeeze out any remaining juice into the saucepan. Discard the bag. Add the sugar and molasses and stir over low heat until both have dissolved. Increase the heat to medium-high and boil rapidly, stirring occasionally, for 15 to 20 minutes, or until a candy thermometer reads 220°F/104°C. Use the "wrinkle test" (page 15) to double-check for a firm set. Skim off any scum. Let stand in the saucepan for 5 minutes before ladling into hot, sterilized canning jars (page 15) , leaving $^1/_4$ inch/6 millimeters of headspace (page 15). Seal. Process the jars in a hot water bath for 5 minutes (page 16). When thoroughly cool, label the jars. Store in a cool, dark place.

Sweet Orange
MARMALADE

THIS IS A HYBRID OF THE CUT-RIND METHOD ON PAGE 39. IN THIS VER-*sion, you slice the citrus fruit, cover it with water, and let it stand overnight in the refrigerator. (Soaking tenderizes the peel and extracts pectin from the peels and pith.) You can make this super-easy marmalade all year-round, as sweet oranges are always available. I've included a lemon in this recipe to give the marmalade some of the tang associated with Seville oranges. If you prefer a sweeter, less acidic marmalade, use all sweet oranges, and increase the amount of sugar from 2 cups/360 grams to 3 cups/480 grams. This marmalade lends itself beautifully to variations with slivered almonds, pistachio nuts, basil or other herbs, and wine or liquor.*

YIELDS 3 CUPS/710 MILLILITERS

2 large navel oranges, halved lengthwise

1 lemon, halved lengthwise

2 cups/360 grams granulated sugar

PLACE THE ORANGE and lemon halves cut-side down on a cutting board, and slice as thinly as possible. Discard the stem and blossom ends of the fruit. Transfer the fruit to a large mixing bowl and add 1 quart/946 milliliters of water. (Don't bother removing lemon seeds; they contain abundant pectin and can be easily removed later.) Cover with plastic wrap and refrigerate overnight.

Transfer the fruit and its soaking liquid to a large, heavy-bottomed saucepan. Bring to a boil over high heat. Reduce the heat to medium-low and simmer, stirring occasionally, for 1 hour and 20 minutes, or until the peels are tender when pierced with a fork. The mixture will have reduced by about one-third.

Add the sugar and stir to dissolve. Continue cooking until a candy thermometer reads 220°F/104°C. Use the "wrinkle test" (page 15) to double-check for set. Skim off any scum or floating seeds. Let stand in the saucepan for 5 minutes before ladling into hot, sterilized canning jars (page 15), leaving $^1/_4$ inch/6 millimeters headspace (page 15). Seal. Turn the jars upside-down for a few minutes to ensure even distribution of the fruit. Process the jars in a hot water bath for 5 minutes (page 16). When thoroughly cool, label the jars. Store in a cool, dark place.

Variations:

SLIVERED ALMOND MARMALADE. Stir in 1 to 2 teaspoons or more of blanched, slivered almonds to your finished marmalade, just before pouring into the jars.

PISTACHIO MARMALADE. Stir in 1 to 2 teaspoons or more of unsalted, shelled pistachios to your finished marmalade, just before pouring into the jars.

FRESH HERB MARMALADE. Stir in 1 to 2 teaspoons or more of chopped fresh basil, mint, or lemon verbena to your finished marmalade, just before pouring into the jars.

Blood Orange
MARMALADE

LOVE THE FLORAL AROMA, DEEP MAGENTA COLOR, AND WINELIKE *flavor of blood oranges. They remind me of southern Italy, where they grow in profusion along with huge, knobby, juicy lemons. This rose-colored marmalade makes a festive gift because of its unique appearance. It goes with everything from the simplest English muffin to a buttery croissant, and benefits from the addition of a teaspoon or so of Campari, Cointreau, or Grand Marnier per cup of marmalade added at the end.*

YIELDS ABOUT 4½ CUPS/1 LITER

4 blood oranges

Finely grated zest and juice of 1 lime

4 cups/720 grams granulated sugar, or more to taste

3 to 4 teaspoons Campari, Cointreau, or Grand Marnier (optional)

SLICE THE TOPS and bottoms off each orange and discard. Slice the oranges crosswise as thinly as possible; then cut each slice into four or six wedges. Discard the seeds. Place the orange wedges and 5 cups/1.2 liters of water in a medium mixing bowl, cover, and let stand for 12 to 24 hours.

Transfer the mixture to a medium, heavy-bottomed saucepan. Bring quickly to a boil, then lower the heat and simmer for 30 minutes, or until the peel is tender when pierced with a fork. Stir in the lime juice and zest.

Measure out the cooked citrus and liquid: to every cup/237 milliliters, measure ³/₄ cup/135 grams to 1 cup/180 grams of sugar, according to your preference of sweetness. Transfer the mixture to a clean, heavy-bottomed saucepan, and add the sugar. Over low heat, stir until the sugar has dissolved. Raise the heat to medium-high and boil for 15 to 30 minutes, or the mixture has thickened and a candy thermometer reads 220°F/104°C. Use the "wrinkle test" (page 15) to double-check for a firm set. Stir in the Campari, Cointreau, or Grand Marnier, if you are using it.

Let stand in the saucepan for 5 minutes before ladling into hot, sterilized canning jars (page 15), leaving ¹/₄ inch/6 millimeters of headspace (page 15). Seal. Process the jars in a hot water bath for 5 minutes (page 16). When thoroughly cool, label the jars. Store in a cool, dark place.

"In the Pink"
GRAPEFRUIT MARMALADE

STORE-BOUGHT MARMALADE IS TOO SWEET FOR US," SAYS MRS. MARY *Vosper of Clifton, Yorkshire, England, who sent me this recipe in response to a notice I placed in her local newspaper, asking for marmalade anecdotes and recipes. Her solution is this good, sharp, cantaloupe-colored marmalade, which goes beautifully on buttered toast or scones, or adds a zesty zip as an ingredient in Curried Chicken Salad (page 121), or other curried dishes.*

YIELDS ABOUT 8 CUPS/1.9 LITERS

2 large pink or Ruby Red grapefruits, stem and blossom ends removed and discarded

2 thin-skinned lemons

$6^{1}/_{2}$ cups/1.1 kilograms granulated sugar, or more to taste

SLICE THE GRAPEFRUITS and lemons in half, squeeze out the juice through a small sieve into a medium, heavy-bottomed saucepan, and reserve the seeds. Using a sharp paring knife and your hands as needed, pull out the white membranes from the rinds, leaving behind only the peels. Place the membranes and reserved seeds in a 15-inch/38.5-centimeter square of double-thickness cheese-cloth. Gather up the corners and tie them shut with kitchen string. Add to the saucepan.

Slice the grapefruit and lemon peel into fine strips; add to the saucepan. Add 7 cups/1.6 liters of water and bring to a simmer over medium heat with the lid ajar. Continue simmering, stirring often and pressing the cheesecloth bag to release the pectin, until the peels turn to mush when pressed between your fingers, $1^1/_2$ to 2 hours. Remove the cheesecloth bag, and when cool enough to handle, squeeze any remaining juice from the bag into the saucepan. Discard the bag. Measure the remaining liquid: there should be 7 cups/1.6 liters; if not, add water to make up the difference or boil until reduced to this amount.

Transfer the mixture to a clean, heavy-bottomed saucepan. Add the sugar and bring to a boil, stirring to dissolve the sugar. Taste and add additional sugar if you prefer a sweeter marmalade. Boil vigorously, stirring constantly, for 15 to 20 minutes, or until the mixture thickens and a candy thermometer reads 220°F/104°C. Use the "wrinkle test" (page 15) to double-check for a firm set. Skim off any scum. Let stand in the saucepan for 5 minutes before ladling into hot, sterilized canning jars (page 15), leaving $^1/_4$ inch/6 millimeters of headspace (page 15). Seal. Process the jars in a hot water bath for 5 minutes (page 16). When thoroughly cool, label the jars. Store in a cool, dark place.

Three-Fruit

MARMALADE

WHILE MANY MARMALADE MAKERS DISAGREE ABOUT EXACT *ratios of fruit to sugar, or combinations of different fruits in their recipes, cooks the world over seem to agree on Three-Fruit Marmalade, which is made from an equal number of sweet oranges, lemons, and grapefruits (or variations using tangerines, limes, or apples). This version was given to me by Turkish food writer Tijen İnaltong. It offers a fine way to use up extra citrus fruit. Legend goes that three- and four-fruit marmalades became popular in Britain during Victorian times when, at the end of winter, housekeepers would use whatever remained in their larder to make preserves. This golden apricot-colored marmalade is mild, clear, and bright, with a slightly granular texture. This recipe yields a large volume, but it can easily be reduced.*

YIELDS ABOUT 8¾ CUPS/2.1 LITERS

1 sweet orange

1 lemon

1 grapefruit

7²/₃ cups/1.4 kilograms granulated sugar

SLICE OFF THE tops and bottoms of the orange, grapefruit, and lemon, and discard. Cut the fruit into chunks; discard the seeds. Place all the fruit in a blender or food processor and add 1 cup/237 milliliters of water. Purée the mixture. Combine the purée and 8 cups/2 liters of water in a large bowl, stir, cover, and let stand at room temperature for 4 hours or up to 24 hours. Stir occasionally.

Place the purée in a large, heavy-bottomed saucepan over moderate heat and cook, stirring occasionally, for 45 minutes. Skim off any floating seeds or scum. Add the sugar, stir to dissolve, and continue cooking for another 30 to 60 minutes, or until a candy thermometer reads 220°F/104°C. Use the "wrinkle test" (page 15) to double-check for a firm set. Skim off any scum. Let stand in the saucepan for 5 minutes before ladling into hot, sterilized canning jars (page 15), leaving $^1/_4$ inch/6 millimeters of headspace (page 15). Seal. Process the jars in a hot water bath for 5 minutes (page 16). When thoroughly cool, label the jars. Store in a cool, dark place.

Variations:

FOUR-FRUIT MARMALADE: Add one peeled and cored apple or one lime to the above ingredients, and follow the instructions as indicated, adding additional sugar to taste, if you like.

AMBER MARMALADE: Substitute one Seville orange for the sweet orange, and add two tangerines. Follow the instructions as indicated.

Shredded Lemon

MARMALADE

I MET EXPERT MARMALADE MAKER DOREEN KAY BY CHANCE, AFTER, *talking with her husband, Brian, in his taxicab in Glasgow, Scotland, many years ago. After extolling her virtues as a cook, he invited me to their home on the Isle of Bute, a short ferry ride from the mainland. It was a beautiful journey on a cool, sunny day, salt spray flying up from the sea. We had a marvelous lunch and tasted many of Doreen's marmalades. She gave me this recipe for a delicate and fragrant lemon marmalade. You can substitute Meyer lemons, which are sweeter and less acidic than ordinary lemons. My friend Susan Presby gave me three* etrogim, *a thick-skinned variety of citron used in the Jewish celebration of Sukkoth, or Feast of the Tabernacles. After the holiday, I used them with basic yellow and Meyer lemons to make a stupendous marmalade. For a special touch, add a teaspoon or more per cup of kirsch or grappa before pouring the marmalade into jars.*

YIELDS 4 CUPS/950 MILLILITERS

6 lemons

Granulated sugar

GRATE THE LEMON zest using the large holes of a box grater, avoiding the bitter white pith. Set aside. Remove the pith with a paring knife and reserve it.

Supreme the lemons by taking a knife and slicing between the membranes to release individual segments, free of any white membrane. Extract the seeds from the lemon segments. Place the pith, membranes, and seeds in a 12-inch/30-centimeter square of double-thickness cheesecloth. Gather the corners together and tie shut with kitchen string. Chop the pulp of the lemon segments roughly.

Place the grated lemon zest, the cheesecloth bag, and the chopped pulp in a medium, heavy-bottomed saucepan. Add 2 quarts/1.9 liters of water. Bring to a boil, then lower the heat to medium and simmer for 1 to 1^1/$_2$ hours, or until the mixture has reduced by about one-half.

Remove the cheesecloth bag; squeeze to extract any liquid into the saucepan. Set a large heatproof bowl on your scale, then pour the contents of the pot into the bowl to weigh it. Transfer the cooked zest back to the saucepan. Measure out an equal weight of sugar and add gradually to the lemon mixture, stirring over moderate heat to dissolve the sugar. Bring to a boil, then cook rapidly for about 30 minutes. Reduce the heat to medium-low and simmer, stirring occasionally, for 35 to 45 minutes, or until a candy thermometer reads 220°F/104°C. Use the "wrinkle test" (page 15) to double-check for a firm set. Skim off any scum. Let stand in the saucepan for 5 minutes before ladling into hot, sterilized canning jars (page 15), leaving ^{1}/$_4$ inch/6 millimeters of headspace (page 15). Seal. Process the jars in a hot water bath for 5 minutes (page 16). When thoroughly cool, label the jars. Store in a cool, dark place.

From left, clockwise: Blood Orange Marmalade (page 49), Cut-Rind Seville Marmalade (page 39), Orange-Pomegrante Marmalade (page 77), Dragon Fruit Marmalade (page 87), "In the Pink" Grapefruit Marmalade (page 51), and Shredded Lemon Marmalade (page 57)

Meyer Lemon, Ginger,
AND MINT MARMALADE

YOU COULD EAT THIS MARMALADE RIGHT OUT OF THE JAR. ITS NOTES *of Meyer lemon, ginger, and garden-fresh mint are delicate and lingering. I use raw cane sugar in this recipe because I find it less cloying than white granulated sugar, but either choice would be fine. For plain Meyer lemon marmalade (delicious in itself), simply omit the ginger and mint. This marmalade would go well with Crumpets (page 177) or warm Oatmeal Scones (page 174), along with a cup of jasmine tea, or use it as an accent to complement cold roasted chicken or lamb.*

YIELDS 2 CUPS / 475 MILLILITERS

4 Meyer lemons

1 (1-inch/2.5-centimeter) piece of fresh ginger, peeled, and thinly sliced

1¼ cups/225 grams natural cane or granulated sugar

Small handful of fresh mint leaves, finely chopped

SLICE THE LEMONS in half lengthwise and, using a paring knife, remove the thick white membrane in the center of the fruit. Use the tip of a knife to pick out the seeds; discard. Cut the lemon halves into $^1/_{16}$-inch/2-millimeter slices; you should have $1^1/_2$ cups/180 grams of lemon slices. (To make up any difference, use regular lemon slices.)

Place the lemon slices, ginger, and $1^1/_2$ cups/355 milliliters water in a small, heavy-bottomed saucepan. Bring to a boil, then reduce the heat and simmer for about 30 minutes, or until the rinds are very tender when pierced with a fork. Add additional water to the saucepan if the water level sinks down too low and there is any danger of burning.

Stir in the sugar and bring back to a boil. Immediately reduce the heat and simmer for 10 to 15 minutes, or until the mixture has thickened and a candy thermometer reads 220°F/104°C. Use the "wrinkle test" (page 15) to double-check for a firm set. Let stand in the saucepan for 5 minutes and add the mint before ladling into hot, sterilized canning jars (page 15), leaving $^1/_4$ inch/6 millimeters of headspace (page 15). Seal. Process the jars in a hot water bath for 5 minutes (page 16). When thoroughly cool, label the jars. Store in a cool, dark place.

Kumquat and Earl Grey
TEA MARMALADE

KUMQUATS ARE NATIVE TO CHINA. THEIR NAME COMES FROM THE
Cantonese kam kwat, *which means "golden orange." They are a symbol of prosperity and a traditional gift at Lunar New Year, which is why they are a common sight in Chinese households and shops at that time of year. The delicate citrus taste is enhanced by Earl Grey tea, which is flavored with oil of bergamot (a type of orange). This marmalade is also delicious made with water instead of tea. If you cannot find kumquats in a specialty produce department, they are available by mail order at www.kumquatgrowers.com or www.lavignefruits.com.*

YIELDS ABOUT 3 CUPS/710 MILLILITERS

$1^1/_2$ pounds/675 grams kumquats

4 cups/946 milliliters Earl Grey tea, brewed at regular strength and cooled to
  room temperature

$2^2/_3$ cups/480 grams granulated sugar

SLICE THE KUMQUATS thinly, removing the seeds with the point of a paring knife. Place the seeds in a 12-inch/30-centimeter square of double-thickness cheesecloth. Gather up the corners and tie them shut with kitchen string. Put the kumquat slices and cheesecloth bag in a medium, heavy-bottomed saucepan; cover with the Earl Grey tea. Let stand at room temperature for 24 hours.

The next day, put the saucepan on the stove and bring the mixture to a boil over moderate heat. Skim off any floating seeds. Lower the heat and simmer for 45 to 60 minutes, or until the mixture has reduced by about one-third.

Add the sugar and simmer for another 15 to 20 minutes, stirring constantly, until a candy thermometer reads 220°F/104°C. Use the "wrinkle test" (page 15) to double-check for a firm set. Skim off any scum. Let stand in the saucepan for 5 minutes before ladling into hot, sterilized canning jars (page 15), leaving $\frac{1}{4}$ inch/6 millimeters of headspace (page 15). Seal. Process the jars in a hot water bath for 5 minutes (page 16). When thoroughly cool, label the jars. Store in a cool, dark place.

Tangerine and Vanilla
MARMALADE

DOREEN KAY FROM THE ISLE OF BUTE, SCOTLAND, ADAPTED THIS *recipe from a delightful little English book,* Jams, Jellies, and Preserves: How to Make Them, *by Ethelind Fearon (1953). It also works well with clementines. The vanilla intensifies the citrus flavors. This recipe calls for soaking the fruit overnight after an initial boil; the process develops the flavors and further softens the fruit peels. If you're pressed for time, you may omit this step, but be sure the fruit peels are very tender after the initial boiling period.*

YIELDS ABOUT 8 CUPS/1.8 LITERS

$2^{1}/_{4}$ pounds/1 kilogram tangerines (about 6)

1 lemon

1 vanilla bean, split lengthwise and halved

$6^{1}/_{4}$ cups/1.13 kilogram granulated sugar

PLACE THE TANGERINES and lemon in a large, heavy-bottomed saucepan and add cold water to cover. Bring to a boil, then reduce the heat and cook over medium-low heat for 45 minutes, or until the peels are tender when pierced with a fork.

Lift out the fruit, reserving the cooking water. Quarter the fruit, reserving the seeds. Pull away the peels from the cooked fruit and slice finely. Using your fingers, pull out the membranes that separate each section of fruit. Place seeds and membranes on a 12-inch/30-centimeter square of double-thickness cheesecloth. Gather up the corners and tie them shut with kitchen string. Place the cheesecloth bag, the peels, and the fruit pulp in a large mixing bowl. Scrape in the seeds from the vanilla bean and add the bean pod. Add the reserved cooking water, cover, and let stand overnight.

Place the mixture in a medium, heavy-bottomed saucepan. Bring to a boil. Add the sugar gradually, stirring with a wooden spoon, until dissolved. Reduce the heat to medium and simmer for 15 to 20 minutes, stirring frequently, until a candy thermometer reads 220°F/104°C. (If you have not soaked the fruit overnight, you may need to cook the mixture for about 1 hour, to further soften the fruit.) Use the "wrinkle test" (page 15) to double-check for a firm set. Remove and discard cheesecloth bag. Skim off any scum. Let stand in the saucepan for 5 minutes before ladling into hot, sterilized canning jars (page 15), leaving $^1/_4$ inch/6 millimeters of headspace (page 15). Seal. Process the jars in a hot water bath for 5 minutes (page 16). When thoroughly cool, label the jars. Store in a cool, dark place. .

The Rise of the British Breakfast

MARMALADE FIGURED PROMINENTLY IN THE RISE OF THE BRITISH breakfast. On a visit to Scotland in 1773, Samuel Johnson wrote, "Not long after the dram [of whiskey], may be expected the breakfast, a meal in which the Scots . . . excel us. The tea and coffee are accompanied, not only with butter, but with honey, conserves and marmalades." In Victorian times, breakfast came to represent the most nationalistic of English meals, a vision of sideboards loaded with platters of fried eggs and bacon, grilled mutton chops and tomatoes, broiled fish, cold game, veal-and-ham pies, silver teapots, and racks of crisp toast, served with butter, jams, and orange marmalade.

This ideal applied to the wealthy classes, of course. The poor subsisted mostly on sweetened tea and dry bread with jam or marmalade, because the price of sugar had dropped low enough to be affordable to everyone.

CHAPTER 4
OTHER FRUIT
Marmalades

As MARMALADE RECIPES TRAVELED WITH BRITISH COLONISTS across the expanding Empire in the late eighteenth and nineteenth centuries, immigrant marmalade makers made use of the local fruits they had at hand. In the United States and Canada, for example, imported Seville oranges were very expensive. But there were plenty of tree fruits such as apples and pears growing wild, as well as New World foods such as cranberries and pumpkins, which the colonists used.

Similarly, the colonists found limes in the West Indies; sweet oranges, kumquats, and grapefruits in Australia and New Zealand; guava and pineapples in India; and sweet oranges, citrons, and pomelos in South Africa. All were used for marmalade.

Modern noncitrus marmalades actually often do contain a bit of citrus— either for flavoring or for their abundant amount of pectin, which aids gelling.

Rhubarb
MARMALADE

RHUBARB MARMALADE IS A CINCH TO MAKE, AND PUTS TO GREAT *use any excess rhubarb you might have in your garden. Its sweet tartness makes it an excellent foil for savory dishes such as salmon fillets or grilled pork chops, and it works equally well in desserts, on its own, or with peanut butter in a sandwich. You can certainly tweak the amounts in this recipe—add more or less ginger, vanilla, and sugar according to personal taste. Rhubarb marmalade will keep for a week in a sealed jar in the refrigerator.*

YIELDS ABOUT 2 CUPS/475 MILLILITERS

1 pound/450 grams (about 4 large stalks) unpeeled rhubarb, washed, and cut into 1-inch/2.5-centimeter pieces

Grated zest and juice of 1 lemon (zest grated on the large holes of a box grater)

1 to 1$^3/_4$ cups/180 to 315 grams granulated sugar, according to taste

2 teaspoons grated peeled fresh ginger

$^1/_2$ teaspoon vanilla extract

Salt and freshly ground black pepper

IN A MEDIUM SAUCEPAN, combine the rhubarb, lemon juice and zest, sugar, ginger, vanilla, and $^3/_4$ cup/180 milliliters of water. Cook over moderate heat, stirring occasionally, for about 20 minutes, or until the rhubarb is tender and the consistency is jamlike. Season with salt and pepper to taste. Transfer to a nonreactive container and let cool to room temperature. Use immediately, or store in the refrigerator for up to 1 week.

Double-Ginger Pear

MARMALADE

PEARS AND GINGER HAVE A NATURAL AFFINITY, AND, WITH ITS USE *of both fresh and crystallized ginger, this marmalade is for true ginger lovers. I like to add a few fresh mint or lemon verbena leaves to the finished marmalade. Because pears don't contain much pectin, this recipe employs a different method: whole, ground lemons rather than grated citrus peels maximize the marmalade's set, and you don't add any additional liquid. (The pears, sugar, and other ingredients will liquefy on their own.) The result is rich and robust. You could do a variation on the classic French dessert* Pears Belle Hélène *by spooning a couple of spoonfuls of this marmalade over vanilla ice cream, and drizzling with hot fudge sauce.*

YIELDS ABOUT 4 CUPS/946 MILLILITERS

2 small lemons, seeds removed and roughly chopped

3 pounds/1.36 kilograms (about 6) Bartlett pears, peeled, cored, and roughly chopped

$4^{1}/_{2}$ cups/810 grams granulated sugar

Grated zest and juice of $1^{1}/_{2}$ lemons

$1^{1}/_{2}$ teaspoons peeled and finely chopped or grated fresh ginger

¼ cup/34 grams diced crystallized ginger

1 vanilla bean, split lengthwise

Fresh mint or lemon verbena leaves (optional)

PLACE THE LEMONS in the workbowl of a food processor and pulse briefly to make a chunky purée. (Do not liquefy.) In a large saucepan, combine the pulsed lemons, pears, sugar, lemon zest and juice, fresh and crystallized ginger, and vanilla bean. Bring to a boil over moderate heat, stirring constantly until the sugar is dissolved.

Lower the heat to medium-low and simmer, stirring occasionally, for about 1 to 1½ hours, or until the mixture has thickened and reduced by approximately one-half, and a candy thermometer reads 220°F/104°C. Use the "wrinkle test" (page 15) to double-check for set. Do not overcook and allow the syrup to get too thick or dark; it will thicken considerably as it cools. Skim off any foam. Remove and discard the vanilla bean. Add a few fresh mint or lemon verbena leaves, if you like.

Ladle into hot, sterilized canning jars (page 15), leaving ¼ inch/6 millimeters of headspace (page 15). Seal. Turn the jars upside-down for a few minutes to ensure even distribution of the fruit. Process the jars in a hot water bath for 5 minutes (page 16). When thoroughly cool, label the jars. Store in a cool, dry place.

Peach and Orange
MARMALADE

THIS MARMALADE EVOKES THE FLAVORS OF SUMMER. ITS SUNNY *apricot color and luscious peachy flavor complemented by bits of sweet orange peel make it a natural partner to any kind of toast, English muffins, biscuits, or scones. It can also be used to line pastry shells for summer fruit tarts. Try to use the tastiest peaches available; the better the peach, the better the marmalade.*

YIELDS 5½ CUPS/1.2 LITERS

2 navel oranges, peeled (peels reserved)

6 large ripe peaches

Juice of 1 lemon

4½ cups/810 grams granulated sugar

CUT THE ORANGE PEELS into ¼-inch/6-millimeter-wide strips. Place in a medium, heavy-bottomed saucepan, and add water to cover by about 1½ inches/4 centimeters. Bring to a boil, then reduce the heat to low. Simmer for about 1 hour, or until the peels are very tender when pierced with a fork.

Skim off any scum. Drain, and cut the orange peels into small diamonds or squares.

Blanch the peaches for 1 minute in boiling water, then plunge them briefly into a bowl of ice water to stop the cooking process. Peel, discarding the peels, slicing the peaches thinly. Cut the orange pulp into rough chunks.

Place the orange peel, peaches, orange pulp, lemon juice, and $1/2$ cup/120 milliliters of water into a medium, heavy-bottomed saucepan. Add the sugar and cook over moderate heat, stirring constantly, until the sugar dissolves. Reduce the heat to medium-low and cook, stirring occasionally, for $1^1/2$ hours, or until the mixture becomes thick and transparent and a candy thermometer reads 220°F/104°C. Use the "wrinkle test" (page 15) to double-check for a firm set. Skim off any scum. Let stand in the saucepan for 5 minutes before ladling into hot, sterilized canning jars (page 15), leaving $1/4$ inch/6 millimeters of headspace (page 15). Seal. Process the jars in a hot water bath for 5 minutes (page 16). When thoroughly cool, label the jars. Store in a cool, dark place.

Orange-Pomegranate
MARMALADE

POMEGRANATES HAVE A MILD, BITTERSWEET FLAVOR. THEIR NUM-erous deep red seeds make a lovely addition to this deep rose-colored marmalade. For this marmalade, you will need one 11-ounce/205-gram pomegranate for its seeds (plastic containers of pomegranate seeds are also available in supermarkets), and a small bottle of 100 percent pomegranate juice. If you wish to make your own pomegranate juice, place the seeds in a blender or food processor and pulse until liquefied. Pour the liquid through a fine sieve or a cheesecloth-lined strainer, using a spoon to press the pulp against the strainer and extract as much juice as possible. Note that pomegranate juice can stain fabric, certain kinds of counters, and wooden cutting boards. It's a good idea to wear an apron and use a plastic cutting board.

YIELDS 3 CUPS/710 MILLILITERS

1 (11-ounce/205-gram) pomegranate, or 1 scant cup/ 122 grams fresh pomegranate seeds

2 large navel oranges, halved lengthwise

1 lemon, halved lengthwise

1 cup/225 milliliters pomegranate juice

3$\frac{1}{2}$ cups/630 grams granulated sugar

SLICE OFF THE CROWN of the pomegranate. Discard. Score the pomegranate into four sections. Break the fruit in half gently by pulling it apart with your fingers. Then break the half into quarters. Place the sections in a bowl of cold water. Separate the seeds from their membranes with your fingers, letting them sink to the bottom of the bowl. Discard the empty membranes and pick out the bits that are floating on the surface of the water. Pour through a strainer, to separate the seeds, which are now ready to use. Set aside.

Place the orange and lemon halves cut-side down on a cutting board, and slice as thinly as possible. Discard the stem and blossom ends of the fruit. Transfer the fruit to a large mixing bowl; add the pomegranate juice and 3 cups/675 milliliters water. (Don't bother removing the lemon seeds; they contain abundant pectin and can be easily removed later.) Cover with plastic wrap and refrigerate overnight.

Transfer the oranges and lemon and their soaking liquid to a large, heavy-bottomed saucepan. Bring to a boil over high heat, then reduce the heat to medium-low and simmer uncovered, stirring occasionally, for 1 hour and 20 minutes, or until the peels are very tender when pierced with a fork and the mixture has reduced by about one-third. Add the sugar and stir to dissolve. Add the pomegranate seeds and continue cooking over medium heat until a candy thermometer reads 220°F/104°C. Use the "wrinkle test" (page 15) to double-check for set. Skim off any scum or floating seeds. Let stand in the saucepan for 5 minutes before ladling into hot, sterilized canning jars (page 15), leaving $^1/_4$ inch/6 millimeters of headspace (page 15). Seal. Turn the jars upside-down for a few minutes to ensure even distribution of the fruit. Process the jars in a hot water bath for 5 minutes (page 16). When thoroughly cool, label the jars.

Cherry
MARMALADE

TINY CUBES OF ORANGE PEEL, ALONG WITH LEMON ZEST AND LEMON *juice, add a citrusy punch to this velvety, dark purple spread. If cherries are not in season, you can substitute frozen cherries, which enable you to bring a taste of summer into your pantry any time of the year. If I have leftover Seville oranges, I chop up half of one orange and add it to the mixture to create another layer of flavor.*

YIELDS ABOUT 2½ CUPS / 590 MILLILITERS

4 cups pitted sweet cherries, or 2 (12-ounce/340-gram) packages frozen sweet cherries, thawed

1 orange, unpeeled, and cut into ¼-inch/ 6-millimeter dice, seeds discarded

Grated zest and juice of 1 lemon (zest grated on the large holes of a box grater)

1½ cups/270 grams granulated sugar

2 teaspoons kirsch (clear cherry brandy, optional)

⅓ cup/23 grams lightly toasted chopped walnuts (optional)

CHOP ABOUT THREE QUARTERS of the cherries roughly, leaving the remainder whole. Place the cherries, orange, and lemon zest and juice in a medium, nonreactive saucepan. Bring to a boil over medium-high heat. Reduce the heat to medium-low and simmer, stirring frequently, for 20 to 30 minutes, or until the orange peel is tender when pierced with a fork.

Add the sugar, stirring to allow it to dissolve. Raise the heat to medium-high and cook, stirring frequently, for 15 to 20 minutes, or until the mixture thickens and a candy thermometer reads 220°F/104°C. Use the "wrinkle test" (page 15) to double-check for set. Add the kirsch and chopped walnuts, if using. Let stand in the saucepan for 5 minutes before ladling into hot, sterilized canning jars (page 15), leaving $1/4$ inch/6 millimeters of headspace (page 15). Seal. Turn the jars upside-down for a few minutes to ensure even distribution of the fruit. Process the jars in a hot water bath for 5 minutes (page 16). When thoroughly cool, label the jars. Store in a cool, dry place.

Left: Orange-Pomegranate Marmalade (page 77), Right: Tangerine and Vanilla Marmalade (page 65)

CHAPTER 5

EXOTIC *Marmalades*

PRACTICALLY ANY FRUIT MAY BE USED TO MAKE SOME FORM OF marmalade or jam. Coconuts, pineapples, bananas, guava, melons, Ugli fruit, tangelos, apricots, red currants, plums, grapes, and bergamot oranges, are all fair game, not to mention certain Asian fruits such as kaffir limes, yuzu, Assam lemons, and Bengal citrons. This chapter's offerings use some unexpected fruit that are not typically associated with marmalade.

Passion Fruit

MARMALADE

I FIRST ENCOUNTERED THIS APRICOT-COLORED MARMALADE, EXOTI-
cally speckled with black seeds, at the gorgeous Kilgraney Country House hotel in Bage-nalstown, County Carlow, Ireland. There, it is served alongside more traditional Seville orange marmalade with their spectacular "full Irish" breakfast.

Passion fruits are odd-looking, egg-shaped fruits which blend wonderfully with citrus fruit. Passion fruits are expensive, and may need to be special ordered. The investment is well worth it, though; this unusual marmalade will have everyone clamoring for the recipe. If you are unable to find passion fruits, substitute dragon fruit (see variation, page 88).

YIELDS ABOUT 4 CUPS/950 MILLILITERS

2 pounds/900 grams (about 6) Seville oranges, halved with seeds reserved

2 lemons, halved with seeds reserved

10 passion fruits, halved, flesh and seeds scooped out with a spoon

5 cups/900 grams granulated sugar

PLACE THE SEVILLE ORANGE and lemon seeds in a 12-inch/30-centimeter square of double-thickness cheesecloth. Gather up the corners and tie them shut

Left: Dragon Fruit Marmalade, page 88

with kitchen string. Place in a large glass or ceramic bowl. Slice the oranges and lemons thinly. Add to the bowl. Cover with 2 quarts/1.9 liters of water, and set a plate directly on the fruit to keep it submerged. Let stand overnight at room temperature.

Transfer the cheesecloth bag and the citrus fruit to a deep, heavy-bottomed saucepan. Bring to a boil over medium heat. Reduce the heat to low and simmer for 45 minutes, or until the citrus peels are tender when pierced with a fork and the mixture is reduced by half. Remove the cheesecloth bag and squeeze out any excess liquid from the bag into the saucepan. Discard the bag.

Halve the passion fruits and scrape out the flesh and seeds with a spoon. Add the sugar to the saucepan and slowly return the mixture to a boil, stirring frequently until the sugar has dissolved. Skim the surface to remove any foam. Add the passion fruit flesh and seeds to the pan. Boil the mixture rapidly for 15 minutes, then simmer, stirring occasionally, for 35 to 45 minutes, or until a candy thermometer reads 220°F/104°C. Use the "wrinkle test" (page 15) to double-check for a firm set. Skim off any scum. Let stand in the saucepan for 5 minutes before ladling into hot, sterilized canning jars (page 15), leaving $^1/_4$ inch/6 millimeters of headspace (page 15). Seal. Process the jars in a hot water bath for 5 minutes (page 16). When thoroughly cool, label the jars. Store in a cool, dark place.

Variations:

DRAGON FRUIT MARMALADE. Substitute 2 pounds of whole dragon fruit for the passion fruits: Slice the fruit in half, scoop out the flesh, and roughly chop. Proceed as directed, using the dragon fruit instead of passion fruit.

Bitter Orange, Rose Water,
AND ALMOND MARMALADE

THIS IS A BEAUTIFUL, ELEGANT MARMALADE, TRANSLUCENT WITH *slivered almonds suspended in an apricot-colored jelly. It evokes the flavorings of North Africa. I find that bottling this marmalade in a hexagonal glass jar (available from www.specialtybottle.com), rather than a plain jam jar, shows it off well, and elevates it from a pantry staple to a very special "gift" marmalade. Rose water is available in specialty food stores and in Middle Eastern markets.*

YIELDS 5 CUPS/1.2 LITERS

3 Seville oranges, about $1^1/_2$ pounds/675 grams, thinly sliced with seeds reserved

1 lemon, thinly sliced with seeds reserved

5 cups/900 grams granulated sugar

$^1/_8$ cup/30 milliliters rose water

$^1/_3$ cup/35 grams slivered almonds, toasted in a dry skillet until lightly golden

PUT THE ORANGE and lemon slices in a medium bowl and cover with 6 cups/ 1.5 liters of cold water. Put the seeds in a small bowl and cover with 1 cup/237 milliliters of water. Leave both to soak at room temperature overnight.

Transfer the citrus slices and their soaking water into a medium, heavy-bottomed saucepan. Strain the soaking water from the seeds and add to the saucepan. Place the seeds on a 12-inch/30-centimeter square of double-thickness cheesecloth. Gather up the corners and tie them shut with kitchen string. Add the bag to the saucepan.

Bring to a boil, then lower the heat and gently simmer the mixture for $1^1/_2$ hours, or until the citrus peel is tender when pierced with a fork. Turn off the heat. Remove the bag of seeds and, when cool enough to handle, squeeze to extract as much pectin into the saucepan as possible. Discard the bag.

Add the sugar and stir over low heat to dissolve. Raise the heat to medium-high, and cook for 15 to 20 minutes, or until a candy thermometer reads 220°F/104°C. Use the "wrinkle test" (page 15) to double-check for set. Skim off any scum or floating seeds. Stir in the rose water and almonds. Let stand in the saucepan for 5 minutes before ladling into hot, sterilized canning jars (page 15), leaving $^1/_4$ inch/6 millimeters of headspace (page 15). Seal. Turn the jars upside-down for a few minutes to ensure even distribution of the fruit. Process the jars in a hot water bath for 5 minutes (page 16). When thoroughly cool, label the jars. Store in a cool, dry place.

Coconut
MARMALADE

JEWISH FOOD SCHOLARS AND COOKBOOK AUTHORS CLAUDIA RODEN *and Joan Nathan both cite this recipe as being of Egyptian origin. It is traditionally made at Passover. This translucent white spread, with a texture somewhat like that of sauerkraut, sings of coconut, sugar, and orange blossom water. It is traditionally eaten on its own with whipped cream, or spread on a matzo. It could also make a terrific filling for cake layers. You can highlight this dish's Middle Eastern flavorings by sprinkling it with chopped raw unsalted pistachios or toasted slivered almonds, and accompanying it with mint tea.*

YIELDS 2½ CUPS/590 MILLILITERS

1 pound/450 grams dried unsweetened coconut flakes

1 tablespoon orange-blossom water

1¼ cups/225 grams granulated sugar

1 tablespoon freshly squeezed lemon juice

¼ cup/29 grams chopped raw unsalted pistachio nuts
  or slivered almonds (optional)

PLACE THE COCONUT in a bowl and sprinkle it with the orange-blossom water and $^1/_2$ cup/120 milliliters of water. Fluff with a fork, cover, and let stand overnight to swell and moisten.

Combine the sugar, lemon juice, and $^1/_3$ cup/75 milliliters of water in a medium saucepan. Bring to a boil, then reduce the heat to low and simmer for 3 minutes. The liquid will be a clear syrup. Add the coconut, and over low heat, bring to a boil, stirring constantly. As soon as it boils, remove from the heat. Let it stand for a few minutes to cool, before pouring it into airtight jars. This marmalade will keep for several weeks in the refrigerator.

Yuzu
MARMALADE

YUZU IS A HYBRID OF AN ANCIENT CITRUS FRUIT CALLED *ICHANG* papeda *and a sour mandarin orange. Native to China and Japan, it has been embraced by American fusion chefs for its floral fragrance and bittersweet lemon-lime-grapefruit flavor. You could substitute kaffir limes or any other offbeat Asian citrus fruit for the yuzu. This marmalade would be nice on toast or ice cream; you could also use it to flavor salad dressings and seafood dishes. Fresh yuzu can be found September through January in Japanese markets.*

YIELD 1½ TO 2 CUPS / 355 TO 475 MILLILITERS

3 fresh yellow yuzu

Granulated sugar

CUT THE YUZU into halves and juice the fruit. Strain the juice through a sieve and reserve. Quarter the remaining halves, and using a sharp paring knife or your fingers, remove the white membranes from inside the peels. Set aside. Remove the seeds and place them in a 12-inch/30-centimeter square of double-thickness cheesecloth. Gather up the corners and tie them shut with kitchen string. Set aside.

To precook the yuzu, place the membranes in a saucepan and fill with water to cover. Bring to a boil, then reduce the heat to low and simmer for 8 minutes. Remove from the heat. Drain in a strainer and discard the liquid. When the membranes are cool enough to handle, chop roughly.

Meanwhile, using a sharp knife, cut each quarter of the yuzu into very thin strips. Place the peel in a saucepan with water to cover and bring to a boil. Lower the heat and simmer for 5 minutes. Remove from the heat and drain with a strainer.

Combine the precooked yuzu membranes and peel with the reserved juice, and weigh. Measure out the sugar to equal half the weight of the combined yuzu mixture.

Place the combined yuzu mixture with the sugar in the saucepan and cover with water until just submerged. Add the reserved cheesecloth bag of seeds.

Bring to a boil. Reduce the heat to medium-low and simmer gently for 15 to 20 minutes, stirring constantly, until the fruit mixture has reduced by about one-third and a candy thermometer reads 220°F/104°C. Use the "wrinkle test" (page 15) to double-check for set. Skim off any scum. Remove and discard the cheese-cloth bag. Let stand in the saucepan for 15 minutes before ladling into hot, steril-ized canning jars (page 15), leaving $1/4$ inch/6 millimeters of headspace (page 15). Seal. Turn the jars upside-down for a few minutes to ensure even distribution of the fruit. Process the jars in a hot water bath for 5 minutes (page 16). When thor-oughly cool, label jars. Store in a cool, dry place.

Banana

MARMALADE

ENGLISH COOKBOOK AUTHOR MAY BYRON OFFERS TWO RECIPES FOR *plain banana marmalade in her book* Jams and Jellies *(1917). I can imagine them as "nursery food" or jam for someone on a very bland diet. Fast-forward to 1998 and to Latin America, where in his book,* Healthy Latin Cooking, *Steven Raichlen includes a recipe for a very tropical-tasting Banana Jam from Guatemala. This recipe is inspired by both authors.*

MAKES ABOUT 1½ CUPS/355 MILLILITERS

3 ripe bananas, peeled and thinly sliced

½ cup/120 milliliters, plus 1 tablespoon orange juice

Juice of 1 lime

¾ cup/135 grams granulated sugar

1 (1½-inch/4-centimeter) stick cinnamon

½ vanilla bean, split open lengthwise

Pinch of salt

PLACE THE BANANAS, orange juice, lime juice, sugar, cinnamon stick, vanilla bean, and salt in a medium, heavy-bottomed saucepan. Bring to a boil over high heat. Reduce the heat to very low and simmer, stirring often, for 15 minutes, or until the marmalade is thick and jamlike. Watch carefully that it doesn't burn.

Let cool, and ladle the marmalade into airtight containers. Once opened, this marmalade will keep in the refrigerator for 3 weeks.

Marmalade Mixology

LEAVE IT TO THE BRITISH TO INCORPORATE THEIR FAVORITE BREAK-fast spread into their cocktails.

Those who may have rushed out of the house without eating their toast and marmalade might consider having a late-morning Breakfast Martini as an eye-opener. It comprises gin, orange marmalade, orange liqueur, and lemon juice. *The Savoy Cocktail Book* (1930) also recommends a Marmalade Cocktail, made from orange marmalade, lemon juice, and gin, shaken, as an aperitif before luncheon.

It was the American general Omar Bradley (1893–1981) who allegedly created his own version of the Old-Fashioned when, lacking fresh orange slices in the battlefields of World War Two, he substituted a dollop of orange marmalade. Voilà—the Omar Bradley Cocktail (bourbon, marmalade, a squeeze of lemon juice, Angostura bitters, maraschino cherry) was born.

My personal favorite marmalade quaff is the PG Tipple, created by Ryan Cannon at the Spotted Pig, New York's enormously popular, Michelin-starred gastro-pub. It's made with Bulleit bourbon, double-brewed fresh mint–steeped PG Tips tea (an English black tea that chef April Bloomfield prefers), lemon juice, simple syrup, and a bar spoon of orange marmalade. Combine all the ingredients, shake, and pour over ice in a highball glass. The marmalade will float to the top of the cocktail.

CHAPTER 6

SAVORY
Marmalades

MORE AND MORE CHEFS ARE IMPROVISING ON THE IDEA OF "marmalade." They are selecting vegetables such as onions, zucchini, eggplant, red cabbage, tomatoes, peppers, mushrooms, and tomatillos and reducing them down to a jamlike consistency, to be used as a side dish or garnish for meat, poultry, and fish.

This is not really a new idea, when you think about familiar savory spreads such as hummus, ratatouille, caponata, and tapenade that are often used as dips or garnishes for other foods.

Savory marmalades work well when spread on a cracker with goat cheese, coarsely ground black pepper, and finely chopped parsley. They're also nice as an hors d'oeuvre: top tiny boiled new potatoes with a dollop of sour cream or crème fraîche, and a dab of marmalade.

Summer Tomato
MARMALADE

THIS RICH, VIBRANT, AND HIGHLY CONCENTRATED MARMALADE *could stand in nicely for the Red Onion Marmalade used in Meatloaf with Red Onion Marmalade Glaze (page 127). Inspired by a recipe from Edith Hunter of Weathersfield, Vermont, it's a nice vehicle for using up garden tomatoes in summer, as it requires a great quantity of tomatoes, which ultimately cook down to a pastelike consistency. Don't even attempt this recipe out of season, when store-bought tomatoes are pale, cottony, and flavorless.*

YIELDS 1 CUP/235 MILLILITERS

$^1/_4$ cup/45 grams granulated sugar

4 small yellow onions, minced

4 pounds/1.8 kilograms firm, ripe tomatoes, peeled, cored, and quartered

$^1/_4$ teaspoon freshly grated nutmeg

$^1/_4$ teaspoon ground mace

Salt and freshly ground black pepper

PUT THE SUGAR in a medium-large, heavy-bottomed saucepan. Cook over low heat, stirring constantly, for 4 to 5 minutes, or until the sugar melts and becomes light brown in color. Add the onions and 3 tablespoons of water. Sauté for about 3 minutes, or until the onion is golden. Add the tomatoes, nutmeg, mace, and salt and pepper to taste.

Bring to a boil, then reduce the heat to medium. Cook, stirring frequently and breaking up the tomatoes with a wooden spoon, for 20 to 25 minutes, or until the mixture thickens to the consistency of ketchup and becomes slightly glossy. Let stand in the saucepan for 10 minutes before ladling into hot, sterilized canning jars (page 15), leaving $1/4$ inch/6 millimeters of headspace (page 15). Seal. Process the jars in a hot water bath for 5 minutes (page 16). When thoroughly cool, label the jars. Store in a cool, dry place.

Red Onion
MARMALADE

MY BROTHER-IN-LAW, JIM CAMPBELL, GAVE ME THIS RECIPE. HE IS *a fantastic cook and regularly hosts large dinner parties seemingly effortlessly. He pairs this savory marmalade with roast prime rib. To round out the meal, he'll often include Yorkshire pudding, spinach soufflé, and honeyed carrots. This recipe works beautifully in Meatloaf with Red Onion Marmalade Glaze (page 127).*

YIELDS ABOUT 2½ CUPS / 591 MILLILITERS

$1/4$ cup/60 milliliters olive oil

6 red onions (about 3 pounds/1.3 kilograms), thinly sliced

$1/2$ teaspoon red pepper flakes

1 cup/180 grams packed brown sugar

$3/4$ cup/180 milliliters cider vinegar

$1/2$ cup/118 milliliters dry sherry

$1^1/2$ teaspoons grated fresh ginger

$1/2$ cup/50 grams golden raisins

Salt and freshly ground black pepper

HEAT THE OIL in a large, heavy-bottomed saucepan over medium heat. Add the onions and red pepper flakes and sauté until golden and tender, about 15 minutes. Do not let them burn. Add the brown sugar, cider vinegar, sherry, and ginger and cook, stirring frequently, until the mixture thickens, about 20 minutes. Add the raisins and cook, stirring frequently, until the mixture is very thick and dark, about 20 minutes. Season with salt and pepper to taste. Let cool thoroughly. Serve at room temperature. This will keep in the refrigerator, covered, for up to 4 days.

The Perfect Slice of Toast

THE PROPER MARMALADE EXPERIENCE IS MULTISENSORY, balancing the crispness of the toast with the smoothness of the butter, and the tooth and tang of semiliquid, semisolid marmalade. For purists, this involves proper toast.

Alexis Soyer (1810–1858), a "celebrity chef" of his day—he cooked for Queen Victoria, fed the English army in Crimea, catered to the gentlemen of London's Reform Club, and wrote many cookbooks—recognized the importance of making perfect toast.

The first recipe in *The Modern Housewife* (1850) is "How to Make Toast." He writes: "Procure a nice square loaf of bread that has been baked one or two days previously (for new bread cannot be cut, and would eat very heavy) . . . and remove its bottom crust with a sharp knife, and cut into slices one-quarter inch thick. Contrive to have rather a clear fire; place a slice . . . upon a toasting-fork, about an inch from one of the sides, hold it a minute, before the fire, then turn it, hold it before the fire another minute, by which time the bread will be thoroughly hot, then begin to move it gradually to and fro until the whole surface has assumed a yellowish-brown color, when again turn it, toasting the other side in the same manner; then lay it upon a hot plate, have some fresh or salt butter (which must not be too hard, as pressing it upon the toast would make it heavy), spread a piece, rather less than an ounce, over, and cut into four or six pieces."

Bread should not be toasted until quite ready to serve, he admonishes. "Any kind of toast that has been made half an hour [ago] is not worth eating."

Tomatillo-Chile

MARMALADE

SWEET, HOT, AND SPICY WITH A TEQUILA KICK, THIS MARMALADE *goes well with Mexican Steak (page 118), Carnitas (page 125), or other South of the Border–influenced dishes. Tomatillos have a tart flavor, unlike typical tomatoes, and are enclosed in a papery husk that should be light brown in color, but not dry or shriveled. Peel off the papery husk and discard it. Rinse the tomatillos before using. When working with chiles, be sure to wear rubber gloves, as the oils and vapors from the chiles can irritate the skin or eyes.*

YIELDS ABOUT 1 CUP/235 MILLILITERS

1 small red cayenne chile

1 jalapeño chile, minced

4 cloves garlic, minced

1 ($3/4$-inch/2-centimeter) chunk of fresh ginger, peeled and grated

$1/4$ cup/78 grams packed light brown sugar

1 teaspoon kosher salt

3 tablespoons finely chopped cilantro

10 tomatillos (about 8 to 11 ounces/225 to 310 grams, depending on size), husked, rinsed, and quartered

1 teaspoon tequila, plus more to taste

PREHEAT THE OVEN to 500°F/260°C.

Roast the red chile on a baking sheet lined with aluminum foil for 10 to 15 minutes, or until the skin starts to blacken. When cool enough to handle, split open the chile, remove the seeds, and peel off the skin. Mince the flesh.

Place the red chile, jalapeño, garlic, ginger, sugar, salt, and ¾ cup/180 milliliters of water in a small saucepan. Bring to a boil, then lower the heat and simmer the mixture until thick, 15 to 20 minutes. Add more water if necessary to keep from burning. Pour the mixture into a blender or food processor with the cilantro and an additional 2 tablespoons of water and blend until smooth. Return the purée to the saucepan with the tomatillos and an additional 2 tablespoons of water and cook over low heat, stirring frequently, until the tomatillos have broken down and become tender, and the mixture has a jamlike consistency, about 25 to 35 minutes. Remove from the heat and let cool. Stir in the tequila. Let cool to room temperature. Transfer to an airtight container, and store for up to 1 week in the refrigerator.

Marmalade in Literature

MARMALADE FIGURED INTO LEWIS CARROLL'S *ALICE'S ADVENtures in Wonderland* (1865), when, while falling down the rabbit hole, Alice takes a jar marked "orange marmalade" off a shelf and then replaces it on another shelf. Metaphorically, "marmalade" was used to depict the dreariness of everyday English life in T. S. Eliot's "The Love Song of J. Alfred Prufrock" (1917). The Beatles' "Lucy in the Sky with Diamonds" (1967), with its memorable "marmalade skies" lyric, uses colorful food imagery to depict a psychedelic LSD trip.

CHAPTER 7

SAVORY *Marmalade* DISHES

JUST AS IT IS CUSTOMARY TO SERVE ORANGE MARMALADE WITH some of the stinkier cheeses, such as Roquefort or Époisses, the savory dishes in this chapter are enlivened by the sweet-tart kick of marmalade. My friend Ellen Flanagan has developed some variations on classic dishes, including *duck à l'orange* and meatloaf, by substituting marmalade in place of such flavorings as oranges and tomato ketchup.

Succulent foods such as pork and duck go especially well with marmalade, and marmalade adds a nice zip to many soy sauce–based glazes and dipping sauces.

Orange-Barbecued
PORK BELLY

TENDER, SUCCULENT, FLAVORFUL, AND ECONOMICAL, FRESH PORK *belly—a staple of Asian cuisine—has become hugely popular in the United States recently. Also known as unsmoked bacon, pork belly is available in supermarkets and butcher shops in slabs or strips. (Ask the butcher to remove its skin, or do it yourself by simply sliding a thin boning knife beneath the skin, and peeling it up and off the meat. You can leave the skin on, if you like a crackly surface.) My friend Ellen Flanagan also uses this marinade and technique with two racks of country-style pork ribs; after marinating the ribs overnight, she oven-steams them on a rack in a roasting pan filled with about an inch (2.5 centimeters) of water, for the same time as for pork belly. Coleslaw and baked beans are perfect accompaniments. Use your favorite orange marmalade.*

YIELDS 4 TO 6 SERVINGS

1 cup/237 milliliters Whole-Fruit Marmalade

2/3 cup/160 milliliters soy sauce

2/3 cup/125 milliliters ketchup

2 small garlic cloves, mashed

1/2 teaspoon cayenne pepper

1 1/2 cups/355 milliliters orange juice

1 cup/237 milliliters red wine vinegar

2 pounds/900 grams skinless pork belly

COMBINE THE MARMALADE, soy sauce, ketchup, garlic, cayenne, orange juice, and vinegar in a nonreactive mixing bowl or in a large resealable plastic bag set inside a bowl. Place the pork belly in the marinade and make sure it is completely immersed. Cover, and refrigerate overnight.

Remove the pork from the refrigerator, and let stand for about 1 hour to bring the meat and marinade to room temperature.

Preheat the oven to 250°F/120°C.

Place a rack in a roasting pan. Place the pork belly on the rack and reserve the marinade. Cover the roasting pan with aluminum foil. Roast the pork, covered, for 3 hours.

Remove the foil and baste the pork with the reserved marinade. Increase the oven temperature to 350°F/180°C. Roast uncovered for about 30 minutes, or until the glaze is caramelized. Watch carefully to ensure that the meat doesn't burn.

Remove the meat from the oven and cut in $^1\!/_2$-inch/1.3-centimeter slices. (If substituting pork ribs, slice between the bones.) The pork belly makes a great sandwich served on ciabatta rolls.

NOTE: You can prepare this dish ahead of time by marinating and roasting the pork belly at 250°F/120°C for 3 hours, as indicated above. Let the meat cool completely and return it to the bowl of reserved marinade. Cover and refrigerate overnight. The next day, bring it to room temperature and finish cooking at 350°F/180°C for 30 minutes. Alternatively, finish the pork on a medium-hot spot on a gas or charcoal grill, and cook for 10 minutes per side.

Duck à l'Orange

MARMALADE

DUCK WITH SEVILLE OR SWEET ORANGE SAUCE IS ONE OF THE CLAS-
*sic dishes in French cuisine. Here, you can use Blood Orange Marmalade (page 49),
Sweet Orange Marmalade (page 46), or Cherry Marmalade (page 81) to create a sumptu-
ous sauce for crispy, tender duck. This dish would partner well with wild rice and baby
greens dressed in a champagne vinaigrette. (To make, combine extra-virgin olive oil and
champagne vinegar at a ratio of 3 to 1. Add a little Dijon mustard, and salt and freshly
ground black pepper to taste. Mix well with a fork or whisk to emulsify.)*

YIELDS 6 SERVINGS

1 (6-pound/2.7-kilogram) or 2 (3-pound/1.3-kilogram) whole ducks

1 teaspoon kosher salt

1 teaspoon freshly ground black pepper

1 teaspoon dried thyme

1 cup/237 milliliters Blood Orange Marmalade (page 49)
  or Sweet Orange Marmalade (page 46)

1 cup/237 milliliters ruby port

PREHEAT THE OVEN to 400°F/205°C. Place a rack in a roasting pan.

Remove any visible fat from the openings of the duck. Use a paper towel to remove any glands from the interior of the duck. Using the tip of a paring knife, pierce the skin all over the duck, at 1-inch/2.5-centimeter intervals. Do not pierce the flesh. Rinse the duck, inside and out, with cold water. Combine the salt, pepper, and thyme in a small bowl. Sprinkle the mixture over the duck and in the cavity. Place the duck on the rack in the roasting pan, breast-side up, and pour 2 cups/475 milliliters of boiling water all over the surface of the duck. The water will render the fat and make the skin crispier.

Roast for 12 to 15 minutes per pound/450 grams. (For a 6-pound/2.7-kilogram duck, this will take about 90 minutes; for 3-pound/1.3 kilogram birds, 45 minutes.) Remove from the oven when an instant-read thermometer registers 155°F/68°C. Tent the duck with aluminum foil and let rest for 15 minutes. The temperature will continue to rise to 165°F/74°C.

While the duck is resting, combine the marmalade and ruby port in a small saucepan. Simmer briefly until it is well blended. Carve the duck, and serve with the marmalade sauce.

Mexican Steak *with* Grilled Vegetables and

THIS SUMMERY DISH GOES WELL WITH WARMED FLOUR TORTILLAS, *shredded lettuce, grated Monterey Jack or Cheddar cheese, and Tomatillo-Chile Marmalade (page 108). A perfect accompaniment would be ice-cold Mexican beer.*

YIELDS 4 TO 6 SERVINGS

STEAK

1 large clove garlic, peeled

1 teaspoon ground cumin

1 teaspoon ground coriander

$1/2$ cup/120 milliliters olive oil

Juice of 1 lime

1 teaspoon puréed chipotle chile in adobo sauce (see page 125)

1 2-pound/900 grams flank steak

Salt and freshly ground black pepper

2 teaspoons vegetable oil, divided

GRILLED VEGETABLES

Reserved marinade

1 yellow bell pepper, seeded and cut into $1/2$-inch/1.3-centimeter strips

1 red bell pepper, seeded and cut into $1/2$-inch/1.3-centimeter strips

1 medium yellow onion, halved lengthwise, then thinly sliced

3 plum tomatoes, halved lengthwise and then each half cut into 4 wedges

Tomatillo-Chile Marmalade (page 108)

PREPARE THE STEAK: With a mortar and pestle or the side of a kitchen knife, make a paste of the garlic, cumin, coriander, olive oil, lime juice, and chipotle purée. Season the steak with salt and pepper to taste. Place the steak in a nonreactive baking dish and cover with the paste. Toss to coat, cover the dish, and marinate in the refrigerator overnight. Turn over several times to evenly coat the meat.

Remove the meat from the refrigerator and allow it to come to room temperature. Wipe off the marinade and reserve in a medium bowl. Lightly brush the steak with half of the vegetable oil. Place a grill pan over medium heat and allow it to get very hot. (Alternatively, prepare a very hot fire in a charcoal or gas grill.) Lightly brush the grill with the remaining vegetable oil.

Grill the steak according to its thickness—4 minutes per inch per side for medium-rare. When the steak is done to your liking, place it on a serving platter, tent it with aluminum foil, and allow it to rest for 10 minutes.

Meanwhile, prepare the vegetables: Simmer the reserved marinade in a small saucepan over medium-low heat for 10 minutes. Remove from the heat and transfer to a medium bowl. Add the pepper strips, onion, and tomato and toss to combine. Let stand for 3 minutes. Place in the grill pan and sauté for 2 minutes, or until the vegetables are crisp-tender.

Slice the steak thinly across the grain. Serve with the grilled vegetables and a dollop of Tomatillo-Chile Marmalade.

Curried Chicken

SALAD

THIS TERRIFIC LUNCH DISH, SERVED IN LETTUCE CUPS, MARRIES *well with either "In the Pink" Grapefruit Marmalade (page 51) or Whole-Fruit Seville Orange Marmalade (page 36). You can use this salad as a sandwich filling on whole-grain bread or a toasted baguette.*

YIELDS 4 SERVINGS

3 tablespoons curry powder

1/4 cup/58 milliliters orange juice

1/2 cup/118 milliliters "In the Pink" Grapefruit Marmalade (page 51) or Whole-Fruit Seville Orange Marmalade (page 36)

3/4 cup/180 milliliters mayonnaise

1/4 cup/60 milliliters plain yogurt

3 cups/420 grams roasted chicken, diced (the meat from 1 small chicken)

1 Granny Smith apple, peeled, seeded, and chopped in small cubes

2 stalks celery, finely diced

2 scallions, white parts only, finely sliced

1/2 cup/70 grams seedless green grapes, quartered lengthwise

Salt and freshly ground black pepper

1/2 cup/45 grams lightly toasted almond slivers

Large, crisp, sturdy lettuce leaves, for serving

IN A SMALL SKILLET over medium heat, lightly toast the curry powder for about 30 seconds. Transfer to a mixing bowl and add the orange juice and marmalade. Let cool to room temperature. Add the mayonnaise and yogurt. Mix well.

In a large mixing bowl, combine the chicken, apple, celery, scallions, and half of the grapes. Toss with three quarters of the marmalade dressing. (If the salad seems too dry, add additional mayonnaise or yogurt.) Season with salt and pepper to taste. Refrigerate for 1 hour.

Drizzle lightly with the reserved dressing and add the remaining grapes and almond slivers. Toss to mix thoroughly. Serve the chicken salad in lettuce cups.

Marmalade-Braised
LAMB SHANKS

CINNAMON, CUMIN, CORIANDER, ONIONS, AND ORANGES ARE MAIN-stays of Moroccan cooking. In this case, Sweet Orange Marmalade (page 49) stands in for the grated orange zest or dried orange peel that often appears in North African recipes. Lamb shanks are the lower ends of legs of lamb. Meaty and full of flavor, they become meltingly tender after long, slow cooking. This lamb dish would go well with steamed couscous and tzatziki, a cucumber, yogurt, and garlic dip. A dry rosé wine would make a fine accompaniment.

YIELDS 4 SERVINGS

1 cup/125 grams all-purpose flour

1 teaspoon salt

$^{1}/_{2}$ teaspoon ground cinnamon

$^{1}/_{2}$ teaspoon ground cumin

$^{1}/_{2}$ teaspoon ground coriander

4 lamb shanks

3 tablespoons vegetable oil

1 large onion, diced

2 carrots, peeled and diced

1$^{1}/_{2}$ cups/355 milliliters dry red wine

2 cups/475 milliliters chicken stock

1 bay leaf

1 cup/237 milliliters Sweet Orange Marmalade (page 49)

1 (15-ounce/425-gram) can chickpeas, drained and rinsed

PREHEAT THE OVEN to 325°F/165°C.

Combine the flour, salt, cinnamon, cumin, and coriander on a large plate. Dredge the lamb shanks in the seasoned flour. Heat the vegetable oil in a Dutch oven or large, heavy-bottomed saucepan over medium-high heat. Sear the meat until it is browned on all sides.

Remove the meat from the pan. Place the onion and carrots in the pan and sauté for 6 to 8 minutes, or until the vegetables are golden brown. Pour off most of the fat that remains in the pan, and add the red wine. Cook over high heat, stirring with a wooden spoon to scrape up any of the browned bits of meat and vegetables that remain in the pan. Lower the heat to medium. Add the chicken stock and bay leaf. Return the lamb to the pan. Bring to a simmer.

Cover and place the pan in the oven. Bake for about 1½ hours, or until the meat is tender. Transfer the pan back to the stove top. Transfer the meat to a bowl and add the marmalade and chickpeas to the braising liquid. Return the meat to the sauce and cook over medium heat for about 5 minutes, or until the chickpeas are heated through. Adjust the seasoning and serve.

Carnitas with Pico de Gallo

THESE TEMPTING MORSELS ARE A BREEZE TO MAKE, AND ARE A PAR-
ticular favorite of children. They are perfect partnered with flour tortillas and pico
de gallo. You can buy cans of chipotle chiles in adobo sauce in the Latin American foods
section of your supermarket. Purée them in a food processor or mash with a fork. Store the
extra in a glass jar in the refrigerator for several weeks, or freeze it in 1-tablespoon portions
to use whenever you wish. Black beans are an excellent side dish.

YIELDS 6 TO 8 SERVINGS

CARNITAS

3 pounds pork shoulder, trimmed
of fat and cut into 1-inch/2.5-
centimeter cubes

1 cup/237 milliliters Sweet Orange
Marmalade (page 46)

1 large onion, finely chopped

1 teaspoon ground coriander

2 tablespoons tomato paste

1 teaspoon puréed chipotle chile in
adobo sauce, plus more to taste

2 tablespoons unsweetened
dark cocoa powder

1 1/2 teaspoons kosher salt

Freshly ground black pepper

2 bay leaves

1 cinnamon stick

5 cloves garlic, minced

PICO DE GALLO

1 cup/180 grams (3 to 4) peeled,
seeded, and diced plum tomatoes

¹/₂ cup/25 grams finely chopped scallions

¹/₄ cup/15 grams finely chopped fresh mint

¹/₄ cup/15 grams finely chopped fresh cilantro

Juice of 2 limes

Warmed flour tortillas, for serving

PREPARE THE CARNITAS: In a large mixing bowl, toss the pork with the marmalade, chopped onion, coriander, tomato paste, chipotle purée, cocoa powder, salt, and pepper. Place the pork mixture in a large, heavy-bottomed skillet, preferably cast iron, or in two smaller skillets in one layer. Add enough water to cover the meat by 2 inches/5 centimeters. Add the bay leaves, cinnamon stick, and garlic.

Bring to a boil, then reduce the heat to very low and simmer uncovered for 1¹/₂ hours, or until the pork is very tender. Check and stir occasionally, and add water if necessary to keep meat submerged. Skim off any scum that rises to the surface. Taste and adjust the seasonings. Continue to simmer, stirring frequently, for another 30 minutes, or until most of the liquid has evaporated. If you want to caramelize the meat slightly, cook for another few minutes.

While the pork is cooking, prepare the pico de gallo: Combine the tomatoes, scallions, mint, cilantro, and lime juice in a mixing bowl. Allow the flavors to meld for 30 minutes. Serve the carnitas with warmed flour tortillas and the pico de gallo.

Meatloaf with Red Onion
MARMALADE GLAZE

MEATLOAF IS THE ULTIMATE COMFORT FOOD, ESPECIALLY WHEN *the weather is cold and damp and you need something hearty to stick to your ribs. This version, topped with a glaze based on Red Onion Marmalade (page 105), goes really well with mashed potatoes and coleslaw.*

YIELDS 6 SERVINGS

6 slices day-old white bread, crusts removed

4 slices/115 grams cooked bacon, cut into small pieces

2 pounds/900 grams ground beef

1 small onion, finely chopped

2 large eggs

1 tablespoon Worcestershire sauce

2 tablespoons tomato paste

1 cup/237 millimeters Red Onion Marmalade (page 105)

$^1/_2$ cup/100 grams ketchup

2 tablespoons soy sauce

PREHEAT THE OVEN to 350°F/180°C.

Place the bread in a food processor with the bacon pieces and pulse them until you have a cup of soft breadcrumbs with finely chopped bacon. Transfer to a large bowl. Add the ground beef and onion. In a smaller bowl, combine the eggs with the Worcestershire sauce and tomato paste. Add the egg mixture to the meat mixture, mix lightly, and form into a loaf shape on a rimmed baking sheet lined with foil.

Place the pan on a flat rack set in a roasting pan, tent it loosely with aluminum foil, and bake for 45 minutes, or until it is firm to the touch and the interior registers 150°F/66°C on an instant-read thermometer. Remove the foil, and bake uncovered for 15 minutes.

While the meatloaf is baking, combine the marmalade with the ketchup and soy sauce in a bowl. Reduce the oven temperature to 325°F/165°C. Pour the marmalade mixture onto the meatloaf. Bake for another 30 minutes, or until the glaze caramelizes.

Glazed Country Ham

GLAZED HAM IS ONE OF THOSE INDISPENSIBLE DISHES THAT IS GREAT
for any large get-together. If you don't want to use a bone-in ham, you can use a 7- to 8-pound/3.3 to 3.5-kilograms spiral-cut ham. (Spiral-cut hams are somewhat more expensive, but they do not require skinning.) This recipe comes via my friend Ellen Flanagan's Pennsylvania Dutch grandmother. She would serve it for Easter dinner with scalloped potatoes, steamed asparagus, and sour cucumber salad. Ellen prefers to double the amount of the glaze mixture and heat the excess with a little chicken stock to serve as a sauce for the ham. The recipe works well with Orange-Pomegranate Marmalade (page 77) or Peach and Orange Marmalade (page 75). A perfect accompaniment would be Buttermilk Biscuits (page 172).

YIELDS 10 TO 12 SERVINGS

1 (8-pound/3.5 kilograms) smoked, bone-in, skin-on half-ham, butt end rinsed and dried

1 cup/237 millimeters Orange-Pomegranate Marmalade (page 77) or Peach and Orange Marmalade (page 75)

1 cup/237 milliliters prepared mustard

1 cup/200 grams packed brown sugar

1 cup/237 milliliters bourbon

$1/2$ cup/118 milliliters orange juice

REMOVE THE HAM from the refrigerator and allow it to come to room temperature; this will take about 2 hours. Place the ham directly in front of you on a countertop. Working on the side of the ham facing away from you, use a thin, pliable knife to make a small, shallow, horizontal incision in the skin at the very top of the ham. Angling the knife toward the skin and away from the body of the ham and working from the top straight down to the bottom of the ham, peel a strip of skin off. Turn the ham to continue to work with it directly in front of you, repeating this process until you have removed all the skin. This will leave a layer of fat. Using the same technique, trim the fat to about ¼-inch/6-millimeter thickness. Score the fat in a diamond pattern, being careful not to make the cuts all the way through to the meat.

Preheat the oven to 325°F/165°C.

In a medium saucepan, combine the marmalade, mustard, brown sugar, bourbon, and orange juice. Stir together over low heat for 3 to 5 minutes.

Rub about half of the mixture all over the ham, including the cut side. Place the ham on a rack in a roasting pan and tent it with aluminum foil. Bake for 2 hours, or until the ham registers 130°F/54°C on an instant-read meat thermometer. Remove the ham from the oven and brush it with the rest of the glaze. Raise the oven temperature to 350°F/180°C. Return the ham to the oven without the foil tent for 20 to 30 minutes, or until the glaze caramelizes.

Remove the ham from the oven, retent it with the foil, and allow it to rest for 20 minutes before carving.

Left: Glazed Ham with Buttermilk Biscuits (page 172) and Orange-Pomegranate Marmalade (page 77)

Chinese Vegetable Dumplings *with*

MARMALADE DIPPING SAUCE

THESE DUMPLINGS, SOMETIMES CALLED POT STICKERS, ARE BEST *prepared in advance and frozen before removing doing a final quick sauté. Although you won't get the instant gratification of making and eating the dumplings right away, you'll have delicious Asian-style dumplings available in your freezer for a super-quick meal or snack any time. The dipping sauce uses Sweet Orange Marmalade (page 46) as a foil for the smoky flavors of sesame oil and soy sauce. Asian dumpling wrappers, not to be confused with wonton wrappers, are available in the frozen food section of many supermarkets.*

YIELDS ABOUT 48 DUMPLINGS

DUMPLINGS

2 tablespoons vegetable oil

1 cup/55 grams cleaned, stemmed, and coarsely chopped fresh shiitake mushrooms

$^{1}/_{2}$ cup/20 grams shredded napa cabbage

$^{1}/_{4}$ cup/25 grams coarsely grated carrots

2 tablespoons seeded and finely chopped red bell pepper

2 tablespoons finely chopped scallions, white parts only

1 ($1^{1}/_{2}$-inch/4-centimeter) piece of fresh ginger, finely grated

2 tablespoons soy sauce

1 tablespoon sesame oil

$^{1}/_{2}$ teaspoon finely chopped fresh cilantro

$^1/_2$ teaspoon finely chopped
   fresh mint

Chili oil (optional)

Fish sauce (optional)

Hoisin sauce (optional)

1 egg white, lightly beaten

1 (12-ounce/340-gram package)
   frozen round dumpling wrappers,
   thawed

6 to 8 green or napa cabbage leaves

3 tablespoons vegetable oil

$^1/_2$ cup/120 milliliters soy sauce

$^1/_2$ cup/120 milliliters mirin or rice
   wine vinegar

2 tablespoons sesame oil

$^1/_4$ cup/58 milliliters Sweet Orange
   Marmalade (page 46)

Tomatillo-Chile Marmalade,
   (page 108, optional)

MAKE THE DUMPLINGS: Heat the vegetable oil in a heavy skillet over moderate heat. Sauté the shiitakes for 6 to 10 minutes, or until soft. Add the shredded cabbage, carrots, and red pepper, and cook for another 2 minutes. Stir in the scallions and ginger.

Add the soy sauce, sesame oil, cilantro, and mint to the mixture. Season to taste with chili oil, fish sauce, or hoisin sauce. Remove from the heat. The mixture will not be completely cooked, as it will continue cooking when you fry the dumplings.

Set the vegetables in a sieve to drain off any excess liquid. Allow to cool for 20 minutes. Transfer to a bowl and stir in the egg white with a fork.

Line a baking sheet with parchment. Lay another sheet of parchment, 16 inches/40 centimeters long, on the counter. Have ready a small bowl of water.

Place four dumpling wrappers on the parchment on your counter. Drop a teaspoonful of the vegetable mixture in the center of the wrapper. Brush the edge of the wrapper with water and seal the edges by folding the wrapper in half and pleating the edges, using your thumb and forefinger.

Transfer the dumplings to the baking sheet, leaving 1 inch/2.5 centimeters between each one. Place the tray in the freezer. Continue filling a few dumplings at a time, then transferring them to the baking sheet in the freezer. Once the dumplings are frozen hard (about an hour), transfer them to a resealable plastic freezer bag and store them in the freezer until ready to use. They will keep, frozen, for up to six months.

When ready to cook, prepare the dipping sauce: In a small saucepan, combine the soy sauce, mirin, sesame oil, and Sweet Orange Marmalade. Add a dash of Tomatillo-Chile Marmalade for additional pungency, if you wish. Cook, stirring, over medium-low heat for 2 to 3 minutes, or until well combined. Set aside.

To cook the dumplings, preheat the oven to 250°F/120°C. Line an ovenproof platter with the cabbage leaves.

Heat the remaining 3 tablespoons of vegetable oil in a large, nonstick skillet over medium heat. Place the frozen dumplings in the skillet, and sauté for 3 minutes on each side, or until lightly browned. Lower the heat to medium-low and pour $1/3$ cup/80 milliliters of water around the perimeter of the pan. Cover the pan and steam the dumplings for 2 to 3 minutes, or until the water evaporates. Place the dumplings on the platter and keep them warm in the oven while you finish cooking the rest of the dumplings. Serve with the dipping sauce.

CHAPTER 8

SWEET *Marmalade* DISHES

NINETEENTH-CENTURY AMERICANS DID NOT ADOPT THE CUSTOM of using orange marmalade as a breakfast spread as readily as the earlier colonists. In fact, it eventually basically disappeared from the American breakfast table altogether. (Hello, grape jelly, strawberry jam, and other sweet spreads.) Instead, marmalade gradually became more used as a decoration on sweet breads, and as an ingredient in baking.

Marmalade is an excellent addition to desserts as it lends moistness to cakes, and flavor and richness to pastries and cookies. It works particularly well in both frozen and heated desserts—perhaps either extreme of temperature highlights its qualities.

Marmalade Tart

I WAS GIVEN THIS RECIPE BY RORY O'CONNELL, ONE OF IRELAND'S *premier chefs and cooking teachers. It is a lovely buttery tart, with a gentle almond flavor sparked by the inclusion of sweet-sharp Whole-Fruit Seville Orange Marmalade (page 36) or Cut-Rind Seville Orange Marmalade (page 39). Serve the tart at teatime with a cup of flowery jasmine tea, or a brisker cup of Earl Grey or Darjeeling tea.*

YIELDS 1 (8-INCH) TART, SERVING 6 TO 8

PASTRY

1 cup/112 grams all-purpose flour

1 teaspoon superfine sugar

Pinch of salt

3$\frac{1}{2}$ ounces/100 grams (7 tablespoons) chilled unsalted butter

1 large egg yolk

FILLING

4 ounces/112 grams (1 stick) unsalted butter, at room temperature

$\frac{1}{2}$ cup/112 grams superfine sugar

$\frac{3}{4}$ cup/50 grams finely ground almonds

1 large egg, beaten

$\frac{1}{4}$ cup/60 milliliters Whole-Fruit Seville Orange Marmalade (page 36) or Cut-Rind Seville Orange Marmalade (page 39)

Softly whipped cream for serving

PREHEAT THE OVEN to 400°F/200°C.

To prepare the pastry, combine the flour, sugar, and salt in a mixing bowl. Cut the butter into the flour mixture until it is the texture of coarse cornmeal. Beat the egg yolk with 2 teaspoons cold water. Add to the pastry ingredients, tossing with a fork until just combined. Add a little more water if necessary to form a soft, not sticky, dough. If the dough is crumbly, knead very briefly on a lightly floured surface. Wrap the dough in plastic and chill for at least 1 hour.

Roll to a thickness of $^1/_8$ inch/.5 centimeter, and place in an 8-inch, loose-bottomed tart pan. Slice off any extra pastry, and crimp the edges. Line the pastry with parchment paper, and fill with dry beans. (This will keep the pastry from puffing up.) Bake for 15 minutes. Remove from the oven, discard the parchment, and save the beans for another use. Let cool on a rack to room temperature.

To prepare the filling, preheat the oven to 350°F (180°C).

Using an electric mixer or a wooden spoon, beat the butter and sugar together until light and creamy, 3 to 5 minutes. Add the almonds and egg. Gently warm the marmalade in a small saucepan over very low heat for about 3 minutes, or until it liquefies. Put through a sieve, and reserve the liquid. Add the bits of orange rind to the mixture and beat thoroughly. Turn the mixture into the tart shell. Smooth the top with a small spatula.

Bake for 25 to 30 minutes, or until golden brown. The tart will still feel a bit soft, but it firms up a little as it cools. Glaze with the reserved sieved marmalade. Serve warm or at room temperature with softly whipped cream.

Steamed Marmalade Pudding

with ORANGE-BLOSSOM CREAM

SWEET AND SAVORY PUDDINGS ARE UBIQUITOUS IN BRITAIN AND *Ireland. In fact, there, the word* pudding *is a generic term for any sweet dessert following a meal. Puddings may be baked, steamed, or boiled, but they are typically cooked in a dish set inside a larger, shallow baking dish or saucepan, which is partially filled with water. This water bath prevents delicate foods such as puddings from burning, drying out, or curdling.*

This warm, comforting, marmalade pudding is traditional in Scotland. Golden, gooey, and topped with thick, orange- or brandy-infused whipped cream, it's a festive alternative for a Thanksgiving dessert. You'll need a 1-quart/1-liter ceramic pudding basin or mold; an inexpensive, English-made, Mason Cash brand pudding basin is available on Amazon.com. Orange blossom water is available in gourmet shops and Middle Eastern grocery stores.

YIELDS 4 TO 6 SERVINGS

PUDDING

Butter for greasing pudding basin

2 cups/225 grams all-purpose flour

2 teaspoons baking powder

4 ounces/112 grams (1 stick) unsalted butter

3/4 cup/130 grams, plus 1 tablespoon superfine sugar

2 large eggs, lightly beaten
with a fork

$^1/_2$ cup/120 milliliters milk

$^3/_4$ cup/177 milliliters Cut-Rind Seville
Orange Marmalade (page 39)

ORANGE BLOSSOM CREAM

1 cup/237 milliliters heavy whipping
cream

$1^1/_2$ teaspoons granulated sugar

1 teaspoon orange-blossom water,
or brandy, whisky, or rum

PREPARE THE PUDDING: Lightly butter a 1-quart/1 liter pudding basin or other ovenproof dish, preferably with rounded sides. Sift the flour with the baking powder into a medium mixing bowl. Cut in the butter with two knives or with your fingers until it has the consistency of coarse cornmeal. Add the sugar. Stir in the eggs. Beat in enough milk to make a soft cake batter that drops easily from a spoon.

Gently spread the marmalade on the bottom and sides of the pudding basin. Pour in the pudding batter. Top with a circle of buttered parchment paper. Then cover the dish with a double layer of aluminum foil, firmly folded over the edges of the basin.

For ease in lifting the pudding, fold a 24 x 12-inch/60 x 30-centimeter length of foil in half lengthwise, then fold it in half lengthwise again. Place the foil strip under the pudding basin so that the ends are easy to grasp, and set the basin on an upturned saucer in a stockpot with a well-fitting lid.

Pour in just enough boiling water to come just under halfway up the basin—any higher and you risk a soggy, boiled pudding rather than a light, steamed one.

Bring the water back to a boil, then lower the heat to medium-low. Cover the stockpot tightly, and keep at a steady simmer for 90 minutes, checking every 30 minutes to see that the water level remains just under halfway up the basin. If the water level gets low, top with additional boiling water. To check if the pudding is ready, unwrap it and insert a skewer into the center of the sponge; it should come out clean.

While the pudding is cooking, prepare the orange-blossom cream: Use an electric mixer to beat the cream into firm peaks. Add the sugar and orange-blossom water. Set aside.

Remove the stockpot from the heat. Grasping the ends of the foil strip, very carefully transfer the basin onto a cooling rack. Let cool for 10 minutes. Run a knife gently around the interior of the mold. Place a plate or serving dish over the pudding dish, and carefully flip the basin upside-down to unmold the pudding. (If it doesn't unmold immediately, try tapping the sides of the mold with a wooden spoon.) Serve with the orange-blossom cream.

Marmalade
ICE CREAM

KNOWN AS CRÈME D'ARCY, A VERSION OF THIS RECIPE APPEARS IN *the Scottish cookbook,* The Practice of Cookery, Pastry and Confectionery *by J. Caird (1809). It typifies the elegance of the Georgian era, in which upper-class households consumed enormously rich meals. Since this ice cream's components are so simple—light cream and heavy whipping cream, egg yolks, superfine sugar, and orange marmalade— be sure to use the best-quality ingredients you can find. A dark, chunky Seville orange marmalade such as Dark Bitter Orange Marmalade (page 44) works very well here, and this ice cream makes a nice accompaniment to Upside-Down Gingerbread (page 152).*

YIELDS 2½ CUPS / 560 GRAMS

1 pint/475 milliliters light cream

3 large egg yolks

³/₄ cup/168 grams superfine sugar

³/₄ cup/177 milliliters Cut-Rind Seville Orange Marmalade (page 39)

¹/₂ cup/118 milliliters heavy whipping cream

SET A MEDIUM SAUCEPAN with about 2 inches/5 centimeters of water over high heat and bring to a boil. Reduce the heat to keep the water hot and set aside.

In a small saucepan over low heat, heat the light cream to just below the boiling point. (Do not allow it to boil.) Remove from the heat. In a mixing bowl, using an electric mixer or a whisk, beat together the egg yolks and sugar until the mixture is pale yellow and fluffy, 3 to 5 minutes. Add the light cream and beat vigorously to incorporate the eggs quickly.

Place the mixing bowl over the simmering water and, stirring constantly, cook until the custard mixture thickens and coats the back of a spoon, about 8 minutes. (To check, draw a finger across the back of the spoon, and if it leaves a trail, your custard is ready.) Do not allow the temperature to exceed 170°F/77°C. Remove from the heat. Add the marmalade, stirring until fully melted; then leave the mixture to cool to room temperature. Refrigerate until thoroughly cold.

Whip the heavy whipping cream until it is stiff. Fold it into the cold custard. Transfer the mixture to an ice-cream maker, and follow the manufacturer's instructions to freeze. Serve immediately for a soft consistency, or return the ice cream to a covered container and store in the freezer for up to 1 week.

Marmalade Meringue

with FOAMY SAUCE

I HAVE ADAPTED THIS AIRY, ETHEREAL DESSERT FROM WHAT'S COOK-ing at Columbia *(1942), a war relief charity cookbook compiled of recipes contributed by Columbia University faculty and their spouses. Warm, light, and cloudlike, it achieves its airy texture through its composition of beaten egg whites, marmalade, and sugar, steamed together in a double boiler. The creamy, rum-laced, accompanying Foamy Sauce contains raw egg yolks, which should not be served to the very young, the very old, or anyone with a delicate immune system. The meringue uses a simple formula of one egg white, 1 tablespoon of granulated sugar, and 1 tablespoon of marmalade per person, enabling you to adjust your ingredients according to the number of people served. Below is a recipe to serve four.*

SERVES 4

MARMALADE MERINGUE

4 large, very fresh egg whites

Pinch of salt

4 tablespoons granulated sugar

4 tablespoons Whole-Fruit Seville Orange Marmalade (page 36) or Cut-Rind Seville Orange Marmalade (page 39)

FOAMY SAUCE

4 large, very fresh egg yolks

$^{1}/_{2}$ cup/62 grams confectioners' sugar

$^{1}/_{4}$ cup/60 milliliters rum or sherry

1 cup/240 milliliters heavy whipping cream, whipped softly

PREPARE THE MARMALADE MERINGUE: Using an electric mixer or whisk, beat the egg whites with a pinch of salt until very stiff. Add the sugar, beating constantly. Gently fold in the marmalade.

Grease the top half of a double boiler, including the inside of the lid, and heat about $2^{1}/_{2}$ inches/6 centimeters of water in the bottom half. When the water is boiling, pour the meringue mixture into the top half. Steam, covered, over gently simmering water for 1 hour, or until the meringue is puffed, pale brown, and firm. Add additional water, if necessary, during the cooking process to maintain water level.

Meanwhile, make the Foamy Sauce: Using an electric mixer or whisk, beat the egg yolks until thick and creamy. Gradually add the confectioners' sugar, beating well. Add the rum and blend well. Fold in the whipped cream.

Spoon the meringue into dessert bowls or goblets. Serve immediately with the Foamy Sauce.

Torta de Regina de Notte

ORANGES, CHOCOLATE, AND HAZELNUTS: WHAT COULD BE A BETTER *combination? This elegant cake, created by chef Ellen Flanagan, is her favorite Passover dessert, as it contains no flour. This cake would round out the most sophisticated of dinner parties. It is fabulous garnished with chocolate shavings or orange slices and accompanied by softly whipped cream.*

YIELDS ONE 9-INCH/23-CENTIMETER CAKE, SERVING ABOUT 8

TORTE

2¼ cups/200 grams ground hazelnuts, plus 2 tablespoons (or breadcrumbs) to "flour" the pan

1½ cups/270 grams granulated sugar

8 large eggs, separated

Finely grated zest of 2 oranges

Juice of 2 oranges

1 tablespoon vanilla extract or hazelnut liqueur

7 ounces/225 grams finely shaved semisweet chocolate

Pinch of salt

Chocolate curls and thinly sliced oranges, for decoration (optional)

Softly whipped cream, for serving

GLAZE

1 cup/237 milliliters Whole-Fruit Seville Orange Marmalade (page 36), Cut-Rind Seville Orange Marmalade (page 39), or Sweet Orange Marmalade (page 46)

1 tablespoon hazelnut liqueur

1 tablespoon orange juice

PREPARE THE TORTE: Preheat the oven to 350°F/180°C.

Lightly butter a 9-inch/23-centimeter springform pan. Dust the bottom and sides of the pan with the 2 tablespoons of finely ground hazelnuts, or substitute fine breadcrumbs. Tap out any excess.

In the bowl of a standing mixer, or using an electric handheld mixer, beat together the sugar and the egg yolks for about 5 minutes, or until they are light-colored and fall in ribbons from the beaters. Add the orange zest, orange juice, vanilla extract, the $2^{1}/_{4}$ cups of ground hazelnuts, and the shaved chocolate.

In a copper or stainless-steel bowl, beat the egg whites and the pinch of salt until they form stiff peaks. Lighten the egg-yolk mixture by folding in one-third of the egg whites. Fold the lightened egg-yolk mixture into the egg whites. Combine lightly but thoroughly. Pour into the prepared pan. Bake for 55 to 60 minutes, or until the cake is firm, but not hard, to the touch and a cake tester inserted into the center comes out clean. Allow the cake to cool on a rack for 15 minutes. Use an offset spatula or the bottom of a tart tin to transfer the cake onto a 10-inch/25-centimeter cake round or serving plate.

While the cake is cooling, prepare the glaze: Combine the orange marmalade, hazelnut liqueur, and orange juice in a small saucepan. Simmer for 3 to 5 minutes, or until the marmalade liquefies. Remove from the heat and let cool to room temperature. Brush the cake with the glaze. Decorate the cake, if you like, with chocolate curls or thin slices of orange. Serve with softly whipped cream.

NOTE: Ground hazelnuts are often available among the flours in supermarkets that stock alternative grains. To prepare them at home, place the hazelnuts on a baking sheet and roast in a 350°F/180°C oven for 5 to 10 minutes, or until their skins start to split. Transfer the warm nuts to a colander and rub vigorously with a kitchen towel to remove their skins. Place the peeled nuts in a food processor and grind finely, but do not overprocess or they will become an oily paste. Store any remaining ground nuts tightly wrapped in the freezer.

Upside-Down Gingerbread

HERE'S AN INTERESTING VARIATION ON THE THEME OF GINGER-
bread. You can substitute Double-Ginger Pear Marmalade (page 73) or any other
marmalade for the Shredded Lemon Marmalade (page 57) used in this recipe.

YIELDS ONE 10-INCH/25-CENTIMETER CAKE, SERVING 8 TO 10

Unsalted butter for greasing the
  pan, at room temperature

1 cup/240 milliliters Shredded
  Lemon Marmalade (page 57)

2$\frac{1}{4}$ cups/315 grams
  all-purpose flour

1$\frac{1}{2}$ teaspoons baking soda

$\frac{1}{2}$ teaspoon salt

1 teaspoon ground ginger

1 teaspoon ground cinnamon

$\frac{1}{8}$ teaspoon ground cloves

1 large egg

$\frac{2}{3}$ cup/155 milliliters blackstrap
  molasses

1 cup/237 milliliters buttermilk

4 ounces/112 grams (1 stick) unsalted
  butter, at room temperature

$\frac{1}{2}$ cup/90 grams granulated sugar

Softly whipped cream or vanilla
  ice cream, for serving

PREHEAT THE OVEN to 325°/165°C.

Butter a 10-inch/25-centimeter cake pan. Line the pan with parchment and butter the parchment. Heat the marmalade in a small saucepan over low heat for 1 to 2 minutes, or until it is soft and semiliquified. Spoon into the prepared pan, and use the back of a spoon or an offset spatula to spread the marmalade evenly around the pan.

Combine the flour, baking soda, salt, ginger, cinnamon, and ground cloves in a bowl. In a separate bowl whisk together the egg, molasses, and buttermilk.

Using an electric mixer, cream the butter and sugar until light and fluffy, 3 to 5 minutes. Add one-third of the flour mixture followed by half of the buttermilk mixture, alternating the dry and wet ingredients until all are used up. Make sure that the ingredients are completely incorporated before adding the next ingredient.

Pour the batter into the prepared pan over the marmalade. Bake for 50 to 55 minutes, or until the cake springs back to the touch and a tester inserted into the center comes out clean. Let cool on a cake rack for 15 minutes; then transfer to a cake plate to cool completely. Serve with whipped cream or ice cream.

Fresh Berries
with MARMALADE CREAM

I HAVE ADAPTED THIS RECIPE FROM JOHANNE KILLEEN AND GEORGE *Germon's fabulous* Cucina Simpatica *(1991). Incredibly quick and easy to make, it is inspired by the filling used in Italian cannoli.*

YIELDS 4 TO 6 SERVINGS

1¼ cups/310 grams whole-milk or part-skim ricotta

½ cup/118 milliliters Whole-Fruit Seville Orange Marmalade (page 36) or other orange marmalade

2 tablespoons semisweet mini chocolate chips (optional)

¼ teaspoon ground cinnamon

1 tablespoon Grand Marnier

¼ teaspoon vanilla extract

Granulated sugar or honey, as needed

2 pints/340 grams fresh berries

PROCESS THE RICOTTA in a food processor for about 1 minute, or until it is perfectly smooth. Add the marmalade and pulse just to combine. Transfer to a mixing bowl. Add the chocolate chips (if using), cinnamon, Grand Marnier, and vanilla extract. Taste the cream and add a little sugar or honey if you want it sweeter. Refrigerate for at least 1 hour, or up to 1 day.

Divide the berries among four to six serving bowls or goblets. Pour the cream over the berries and serve.

Schnecken

SCHNECKEN MEANS "SNAILS" IN GERMAN, AND THESE COILED LITTLE *pastries are irresistible with a cup of tea or coffee. This recipe was adapted from an heirloom "Gishnitz" recipe—a traditional nuts and marmalade–filled jelly roll, which a family friend, Lucille Brown, inherited from her Austrian grandmother, Fannie Durst Kapner. These individual schnecken can be frozen unbaked for later use. Wrap the four unsliced jelly rolls in foil, then place in a plastic bag and freeze. To bake, slice the frozen schnecken, place on a foil-lined baking sheet (or in muffin tins), and bake as indicated below.*

YIELDS 24 STANDARD OR 64 MINI SCHNECKEN

DOUGH

4 cups/560 grams all-purpose flour

1 cup/160 grams granulated sugar

2 teaspoons baking powder

Pinch of salt

Finely grated zest and juice of 1 lemon

4 large eggs

4 ounces/112 grams (1 stick), plus
   2 tablespoons unsalted butter, at
   room temperature

FILLING

2 tablespoons unsalted butter,
   softened

$^1/_2$ cup/118 milliliters orange
   marmalade (thinner is better)

2 cups/240 grams golden raisins

1$^1/_2$ cups/150 grams, plus 2 tablespoons finely chopped walnuts,
   lightly toasted

$^1/_2$ teaspoon ground cinnamon

Finely grated zest of 1 lemon

2 tablespoons granulated sugar

PREPARE THE SCHNECKEN: Preheat the oven to 350°F/180° C. Lightly butter 24 standard or 64 mini-muffin tins.

In a medium mixing bowl, combine the flour, sugar, baking powder, salt, and grated lemon zest. In a separate bowl, whisk the lemon juice and eggs. Using a pastry cutter or your fingers, cut the butter into the dry ingredients until it resembles coarse cornmeal. Add the egg mixture. Mix lightly just until all ingredients are combined. Gather up into a ball. Divide the dough into four pieces, wrap each separately in plastic wrap, and chill in the refrigerator for about 1 hour.

Fill the schnecken: On a floured board, roll out each piece of dough into a rectangle about $1/4$ inch/6 millimeters thick by 4 x 8 inches/10 x 20 centimeters. Using a dry pastry brush, brush off the excess flour. With the long side toward you, brush each rectangle with one fourth of the softened butter, then spread with one fourth of the marmalade.

In a mixing bowl, combine the raisins, $1^1/2$ cups/150 grams of the walnuts, cinnamon, and lemon zest. Sprinkle the mixture evenly over each rectangle. Roll each rectangle, starting from the long end, like a jelly roll.

Slice each roll into $1^1/2$-inch/4 centimeter pieces and, as you slice, place each piece in the prepared muffin tins. (For mini schnecken, slice the jelly rolls into $1/2$-inch/1.3-centimeter pieces.) Sprinkle lightly with the remaining 2 tablespoons of walnuts and the sugar. Bake for 20 to 25 minutes for mini schnecken, and 30 to 35 minutes for standard schnecken, or until golden and aromatic. Serve either hot or at room temperature with Earl Grey or Orange Pekoe tea, or coffee.

Rugelach *with* Cherry Marmalade
AND CHOCOLATE DRIZZLE

THESE MINIATURE CRESCENTS, MADE WITH A TENDER CREAM cheese dough, can be flavored in many imaginative ways. *Substitute Shredded Lemon Marmalade (page 57); Peach and Orange Marmalade (page 75); or Bitter Orange, Rose Water, and Almond Marmalade (page 89) for the Cherry Marmalade (page 81) used in this recipe. Or revisit a traditional Eastern European filling of finely chopped raisins, walnuts, cinnamon, and sugar.*

YIELDS ABOUT 30 RUGELACH

8 ounces/225 grams (2 sticks), plus 4 tablespoons/55 grams unsalted butter, at room temperature, divided

8 ounces/225 grams cream cheese, at room temperature

2 cups/280 grams all-purpose flour

$^1/_2$ teaspoon salt

12 ounces/360 grams Cherry Marmalade (page 81), pulsed in a food processor to finely chop the cherries

1 cup/100 grams finely chopped pecans or hazelnuts

1 large egg

2 ounces/60 grams semisweet chocolate, roughly chopped

USING AN ELECTRIC mixer, cream the 8 ounces/225 grams of butter for 3 to 5 minutes, until light and fluffy. Beat in the cream cheese and blend well. Combine the flour and salt. In $^1/_2$-cup/70-gram measures, add the flour mixture to the butter mixture. Use a spatula to scrape down the sides of the bowl. Divide the dough into four pieces and flatten each into a disk. Wrap the dough in plastic wrap and refrigerate for at least 1 hour or overnight.

Preheat the oven to 375°F/190°C.

Line a baking sheet with parchment paper. Prepare the rugelach filling by combining the marmalade and the pecans. Prepare an egg wash for the cookies by lightly beating the egg with 2 tablespoons of water in a small bowl. Pass the egg mixture through a strainer to ensure that it is evenly mixed.

Unwrap one of the disks of dough. On a floured board, roll out the dough into a thin 10-inch/25-centimeter round. Brush any extra flour off the dough with a dry pastry brush. Spread the circle with one quarter of the marmalade. Lightly sprinkle the circle with one quarter of the ground nuts. Using a pizza wheel or knife, cut each round like a cake into six triangular wedges. Starting at the wide end, roll up the wedges tightly. Curve the ends of the cookies to make them curve into a "smile."

Place each wedge, point side down, on the baking sheet, leaving 2 to 3 inches/5 to 8 centimeters' space between them. Dip a clean pastry brush into the egg wash and lightly coat the cookies. Bake for 16 to 18 minutes, or until golden and fragrant. Transfer the entire parchment paper onto a wire rack and allow the cookies to cool completely.

In a small saucepan melt together the chocolate and the remaining 4 tablespoons/60 grams of butter. Stir until smooth. Using a paper or plastic pastry cone, or the tines of a fork, drizzle the chocolate over the cooled cookies and allow the chocolate to cool completely.

Marmalade Drops

HAVE ADAPTED THIS RECIPE FROM THE *JOY OF COOKING* BY IRMA *S. Rombauer and Marion Rombauer Becker (1964 edition), by adding a bit of grated lemon zest, cinnamon, and nutmeg to jazz it up. Not that it really needs jazzing—this is the quintessential old-fashioned cookie that is always perfect with a cup of tea or a glass of iced tea or lemonade.*

YIELDS ABOUT 48 (2-INCH/5-CENTIMETER) COOKIES

5 tablespoons/70 grams unsalted butter, at room temperature

$^2/_3$ cup/120 grams granulated sugar

1 large egg

$^1/_2$ cup/118 milliliters Whole-Fruit Seville Orange Marmalade (page 36) or Cut-Rind Seville Orange Marmalade (page 39)

1 teaspoon finely grated lemon or orange zest

$^1/_2$ teaspoon freshly grated nutmeg

$^1/_2$ teaspoon ground cinnamon

$1^1/_2$ cups/270 grams all-purpose flour

$1^1/_4$ teaspoons baking powder

PREHEAT THE OVEN to 375°F/190°C. Grease a baking sheet or line it with parchment paper.

In a medium mixing bowl, using an electric mixer or a wooden spoon, beat the butter until soft and fluffy, 5 to 6 minutes. Add the sugar gradually and beat until light and creamy. Beat in the egg, marmalade, and zest. Combine the nutmeg, cinnamon, flour, and baking powder in a second medium mixing bowl. Add to the butter mixture. If the batter seems too dry, add a little more marmalade; if it seems too moist, add a bit more flour. Drop by teaspoonfuls onto the prepared baking sheet. Bake for 8 to 10 minutes, or until the cookies are golden. Let cool on a rack before serving.

Clockwise from left: "In the Pink" Grapefruit Marmalade (page 51), Yuzu Marmalade (page 94), Tangerine and Vanilla Marmalade (page 65), and Cut-Rind Seville Orange Marmalade (page 39).

CHAPTER 9

BREADS
TO GO WITH
Marmalade

THE BREADS IN THIS CHAPTER ARE HOMELY AND TRADITIONAL. They would not be out of place in an Irish farmhouse, warmed by a smoky peat fire and plenty of *craic* (good fun).

Baked Boxty

"Boxty on the griddle,
Boxty on the pan,
If you can't bake boxty,
Sure you'll never get a man!"

SO GOES A TRADITIONAL FOLK RHYME IN IRELAND, WHERE BOXTY IS *a smooth-textured potato bread made from grated raw potato, cooked mashed potatoes, and flour. Different versions are either cooked as griddlecakes, boiled as dumplings, or baked in loaves. I was given this recipe by Pádraic Óg Gallagher, owner of the famous Gallagher's Boxty House restaurant in Temple Bar in Dublin. He suggests using a floury potato such as Yukon Gold, and recommends allowing the baked loaf to rest in the refrigerator overnight, then griddling it or toasting it, and serving it with plenty of butter and Whole-Fruit Seville Orange Marmalade (page 36), alongside bacon and eggs.*

YIELDS 2 LOAVES

1 pound/450 grams Yukon Gold potatoes, peeled

4 tablespoons/55 grams salted butter

$2^3/_4$ cups/320 grams all-purpose flour

1 pound/450 grams cooked mashed potatoes

$1^1/_2$ tablespoons salt

PREHEAT THE OVEN to 350°F/180°C. Butter two 1-pound/450-gram loaf pans.

Grate the raw potatoes onto a clean cotton dishcloth; draw up the corners and twist into a bag. Squeeze as much liquid as possible into a mixing bowl. Let the liquid stand for 20 minutes. Gently pour off the liquid, but keep the starch that has settled into the bottom of the bowl.

In a mixing bowl, using your fingers or a pastry cutter, cut the butter into the flour until it resembles cornmeal. Add the grated raw potatoes and mashed potatoes, mixing with a wooden spoon to make a floury dough. Mix in the reserved starch and the salt. Turn onto a floured board and knead for 3 to 4 minutes, or until the dough is smooth. (Alternatively, you can use an electric mixer with a dough hook.) Do not overknead as this will produce a heavy, dense loaf. Divide the dough in half, and shape each into a loaf. Place each loaf into a prepared loaf pan. Slash an X into each loaf with the point of a knife.

Bake for 50 minutes, or until the bread is golden brown. Remove from the oven and let cool on a wire rack. When thoroughly cool, wrap each loaf in plastic wrap and store in the refrigerator overnight. Slice into 1-inch/2.5-centimeter slices, and cook on a buttered griddle or in a heavy skillet, or toast in a toaster, for a few minutes, until the cut sides of the loaf are golden brown. Serve warm.

NOTE: The bread will keep well, wrapped in plastic wrap, in the refrigerator for 4 or 5 days. You may slice and fry it as you need it.

Brown Soda Bread

MY GOOD FRIEND ELLEN FLANAGAN'S RECIPE FOR THIS IRISH MAIN-
*stay is the real deal: crisp crust, tender, moist interior and a wheaty, nutty flavor.
She prefers Brownulated sugar (a free-flowing light brown sugar available in the baking
section of your supermarket) instead of packed brown sugar because it stores well, does not
get hard, and blends really well with the other dry ingredients in this recipe. For a delec-
table teatime treat, spread a slice of this bread with Gorgonzola and a dollop of Cut-Rind
Seville Orange Marmalade (page 39) or Aromatic Orange-Apple-Ginger Marmalade
(page 32) and chopped, toasted hazelnuts. In fact, any marmalade is great with this bread,
as is good plain butter.*

YIELDS TWO 6-INCH/15-CENTIMETER ROUND LOAVES

2 cups/240 grams whole wheat flour

2 cups/240 grams all-purpose flour

3 tablespoons Brownulated or packed
light brown sugar

1 teaspoon salt

1 teaspoon baking powder

1 teaspoon baking soda

2 cups/475 milliliters buttermilk

PREHEAT THE OVEN to 450°F/230°C.

In a large bowl, combine the whole wheat flour, white flour, brown sugar, salt, baking powder, and baking soda. Mix well. Make a well in the center of the dry ingredients and add the buttermilk. Incorporate all the flour into the buttermilk, using your hands or a wooden spoon. If the mixture seems too dry, add a splash more buttermilk.

Turn the dough out onto a floured board and knead lightly for about 3 minutes. Divide the dough in half and form into two disks about 6 inches/15 centimeters wide and 2 inches/5 centimeters high. Place onto a lightly buttered baking sheet and slash an X on the top of the loaves with a sharp knife.

Bake for 15 minutes; then reduce the oven temperature to 400°F/205°C. Bake for another 20 minutes, or until the crust is firm. Let cool on a rack for about 15 minutes before slicing. This bread is best eaten the same day it is prepared.

Buttermilk Biscuits

THESE SOFT, MELTINGLY TENDER BISCUITS GO WONDERFULLY WITH *Peach and Orange Marmalade (page 75), topped with thinly sliced Glazed Country Ham (page 129).*

YIELDS ABOUT TEN 2-INCH/5-CENTIMETER BISCUITS

4 ounces/112 grams (1 stick), plus 2 tablespoons unsalted butter, divided

2¹/₂ cups/312 grams sifted all-purpose flour

1 tablespoon baking powder

1 teaspoon salt

1 cup/237 milliliters, plus 2 tablespoons cold buttermilk

PREHEAT THE OVEN to 425°F/220°C. Grease a baking pan or line it with parchment paper.

With a sharp knife, cut 4 ounces/112 grams of the butter into ¹/₄-inch/6-millimeter cubes. Wrap in plastic wrap and place in the freezer for 20 minutes. Combine the flour, baking powder, and salt in a mixing bowl. Add the frozen butter to the flour mixture. Using your fingers or a pastry cutter, cut the butter into the flour until it resembles cornmeal. Alternatively, pulse the flour with the butter in a food processor until crumbly. Turn out into a bowl. Using a fork, stir in the buttermilk just until the ingredients form a soft dough. Knead the dough three or four turns on a lightly floured surface. Roll into a 5 x 10-inch/13 x 26-centimeter rectangle.

Form the biscuits with a 2-inch/5-centimeter biscuit cutter. Place 2 inches/5 centimeters apart on the prepared baking pan. Melt the remaining 2 tablespoons of butter and brush it onto the biscuits. Bake the biscuits on the top shelf of the oven for 12 to 18 minutes, or until they are golden and fragrant. Let cool briefly on a wire rack.

Oatmeal Scones

MY FRIEND BIDDY WHITE LENNON, A WELL-KNOWN IRISH ACTRESS-*turned-food writer, gave me this recipe for these homey griddle scones, which go well with butter and marmalade. The best way to eat these scones is hot from the griddle.*

YIELDS 8 SERVINGS

2^1/$_2$ cups/590 milliliters buttermilk

1^1/$_4$ cups/150 grams finely ground oatmeal (available in health-food stores, or grind whole oats in a food processor or coffee grinder to a fine consistency)

^{3}/$_4$ cup/90 grams all-purpose flour

1 teaspoon salt

1 teaspoon baking soda

1 large egg

Milk, as needed for thinning the batter

2 tablespoons unsalted butter, at room temperature

THE DAY BEFORE you plan to serve the scones, stir together the buttermilk and ground oatmeal in a medium bowl. Cover with plastic wrap and let stand overnight at room temperature.

Just before cooking, sift together the flour, salt, and baking soda, and add them to the oatmeal mixture. Add the egg and just enough milk to make a batter that is a little thinner than you would use for ordinary pancakes. Butter a griddle or heavy skillet, and heat over medium heat. When it is hot, drop in tablespoonfuls of the batter, well spaced to prevent them from running together, onto the griddle.

Cook for about 5 minutes per side, or until the scones have risen, are covered in bubbles on the upper side, and are golden brown underneath. Serve immediately, or keep covered in a clean kitchen towel to allow them to stay warm.

Crumpets

THERE IS NOTHING MORE TRADITIONAL FOR AFTERNOON TEA THAN *these yeasty little griddle cakes, their surface dotted with tiny holes, all the better for absorbing lots of butter and marmalade. This recipe calls for both all-purpose white flour and bread flour. The difference is that white all-purpose flour is blended from hard and soft wheat, with a protein content of 10 to 12 percent, while bread flour is made from blends of hard wheat only, and contains 12 to 14 percent protein. The combination of flours helps achieve a better rise.*

YIELDS 16 CRUMPETS

1 cup/237 milliliters whole or low-fat milk

1 teaspoon granulated sugar

$^1/_4$ ounce/8 grams (1 envelope) active dry yeast

2 cups/280 grams bread flour

2 cups/240 grams all-purpose flour

1 tablespoon salt

2 tablespoons vegetable oil

$^1/_2$ teaspoon baking soda

$^2/_3$ cup/157 milliliters of warm water

Extra oil or butter for greasing the crumpet or English muffin rings

IN A MEDIUM SAUCEPAN, gently warm the milk, sugar, and 1 cup/237 milliliters of water to about 100°F/38°C. Remove from the heat. Ladle about $^1/_2$

cup/120 milliliters of the liquid into a small bowl and add the yeast. Stir to combine. Set aside in a warm place for about 10 minutes, until bubbly.

Combine the bread flour, all-purpose flour, and salt in a large mixing bowl. Quickly add the yeast mixture followed by the remaining milk mixture and the vegetable oil. Mix the batter vigorously with a wooden spoon until it is smooth and elastic. Cover the bowl with a clean kitchen towel and leave it to rise in a warm place for $1^{1}/_{2}$ to 2 hours, or until the surface is covered with bubbles.

Punch down the batter with a wooden spoon. For the second mixing, dissolve the baking soda in the warm water, and stir this into the batter. Cover the bowl again, and let rise in a warm place for 30 minutes.

Preheat the oven to 200°F/95°C.

Heat a griddle or large, heavy skillet over moderate heat for 2 minutes. Grease as many crumpet or English muffin rings (about $3^{1}/_{2}$ inches/9 centimeters in diameter and 1 inch/2.5 centimeters deep) that will easily fit on the griddle or in the skillet. (You can also use round cookie or biscuit cutters.) Place the rings on the griddle or skillet, and reduce the heat to low; allow to heat for 5 minutes. Pour enough batter into each ring to come almost to the top. Continue cooking over low heat until the top of the crumpet forms a skin, 7 to 10 minutes. There should be lots of tiny holes on the surface. (If not, your batter may be a little too thick; add a little warm water before cooking the next batch.) The underside should be smooth and golden in color.

Slip off the rings and use a spatula to flip the crumpets over. Cook for 2 to 3 minutes on the second side, to brown the tops. Keep this batch warm in a covered dish in the oven, while you prepare the rest of the crumpets. Serve immediately, or alternatively, allow the crumpets to cool, then split and toast them.

Marmalade Sandwiches

MARMALADE SANDWICHES ARE THE STAPLE FOOD OF PADDINGTON Bear, the beloved English children's book character, who in Michael Bond's story, was found in London's Paddington Station. He keeps them under his jacket "in case of emergencies." Marmalade and bacon sandwiches, to me, are even better. Simply fry or microwave some bacon until it is crisp. Place between slices of well-buttered toast on which you have also spread a liberal amount of marmalade. Other sandwich combinations include orange marmalade, peanut butter, and bananas on whole wheat toast; membrillo and Manchego cheese on a water biscuit; and lemon marmalade with fresh mint leaves and cold lamb on a whole-grain roll. You can do a lovely variation on Ploughman's Lunch by toasting, splitting, and buttering a hero roll. Spread one cut side of the toasted roll with Dijon mustard, and the other with orange marmalade. Sprinkle shredded Cheddar cheese on one of the sandwich halves, and press the halves together. Serve with potato chips and gherkins.

Popovers

POPOVERS GOT THEIR NAME BECAUSE OF THEIR TENDENCY TO SWELL *over the sides of the tins or cups while they are being baked. These hollow, egg-rich muffins are wonderful with butter, honey, or marmalade for breakfast or afternoon tea, and equally impressive as an accompaniment to roasted meats or poultry at dinner. (Popovers closely resemble Yorkshire pudding.) There's no trick to achieving their light, billowy quality—just be sure not to open the oven door while they are baking or the popovers will collapse.*

YIELDS 6 TO 8 POPOVERS, DEPENDING ON THE SIZE OF MUFFIN TINS

Unsalted butter, as needed

6 large eggs

1 cup/237 milliliters milk

1 cup/140 grams sifted
all-purpose flour

$^1/_4$ teaspoon salt

PREHEAT THE OVEN to 425° F/220°C.

Butter six large or eight medium muffin tin cups or custard cups generously. Place in the oven to melt the butter. Meanwhile, beat the eggs well in a medium mixing bowl. Add the milk, flour, and salt, and beat until just blended.

Remove the muffin cups from the oven and fill three-quarters full with the batter. Place the popovers on the center rack in the oven. Bake for 30 to 35 minutes until puffed and brown. Do not open the oven door while the popovers are baking, or the popovers will collapse! Serve immediately.

Focaccia

FOCACCIA IS A DELICIOUS ITALIAN FLATBREAD, A TERRIFIC BASE FOR
*sandwiches or on its own, dipped in a good olive oil. You can make a super-easy
hors d'oeuvre by cutting the bread into 3-inch/7.5-centimeter squares, spreading it with
Summer Tomato Marmalade (page 102), and topping it with a dollop of ricotta cheese
and a chiffonade of fresh basil. Or spread the squares with a thin layer of Dijon mustard
and Dark Bitter Orange Marmalade (page 44), and top with a square of Cheddar cheese
and a sweet pickle chip. This recipe works best if you have a powerful standing electric
mixer equipped with a dough hook.*

YIELDS 1 (13 X 18-INCH/33 X 45.5 CENTIMETER) FLATBREAD

2 ($^3/_4$ ounce/21 gram) packages
active dry yeast

8 cups/1 kilogram all-purpose flour

2 tablespoons salt

$^3/_4$ cup/45 grams granulated sugar,
plus more as needed

$^1/_2$ cup/120 milliliters, plus 1 tablespoon virgin olive oil, divided, plus
more to oil the bowl

2 tablespoons dried oregano

PROOF THE YEAST in $2^2/_3$ cups/635 milliliters of warm (104°F/41°C) water
until foamy. If the yeast does not foam, add 1 teaspoon of the sugar and stir gen-

tly; it should bubble on the surface of the water. In the bowl of a standing mixer, using the wire whisk attachment, combine the flour, salt, and sugar. Slowly pour the yeast mixture around the edge of the mixing bowl into the flour. Pour in the $1/2$ cup/120 milliliters of olive oil the same way. If the mixture appears dry, drizzle in a little more olive oil until it is moist enough to mix well.

Switch to the dough hook. Knead for 5 to 10 minutes, or until the dough is soft and pliable. If the dough climbs up the dough hook, stop the mixer and pull it back into the bowl and continue to knead. Lightly oil a large bowl with olive oil. Place the dough in the bowl and cover with a kitchen towel. Place the bowl in a warm place and let the dough rise for about 1 to $1^1/2$ hours, or until doubled in bulk.

Preheat the oven to 400°F/205°C. Oil an 18 x 13-inch/45.5 x 33-centimeter baking sheet.

Punch down the dough and press it onto the prepared baking sheet. Let rise for 15 minutes. Brush with the 1 tablespoon of olive oil and sprinkle the oregano on top. Bake for 25 to 30 minutes, or until golden brown. To be sure that the focaccia is done, lift up the bread and check that the bottom is light gold. Remove from the pan immediately and allow the focaccia to cool on a wire rack until it is cool enough to handle.

Index